My Village – My World

My Village – My World

John M. Feehan

Foreword
by
John B. Keane

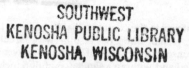

MERCIER PRESS

The Mercier Press
P.O. Box 5, 5 French Church Street, Cork
24 Lower Abbey Street, Dublin 1

941.5
F32

© Estate of John M. Feehan 1992

A CIP record for this book is available from the British Library.

ISBN 1 85635 026 6

Printed in Ireland by Colour Books Ltd.

CONTENTS

CONTENTS

Foreword

The author of this book, John M. Feehan, was a constant companion for thirty years. I had often suggested to him that he write his memoirs. He never did. What he did write was something far less pretentious but infinitely more important than mere memoirs. He had left behind a legacy of wit, laughter and wisdom in *My Village – My World*.

I have never laughed so much throughout the course of any book-reading. Spilling from the pages are hilarious accounts of the fantastic activities relating to ancient outdoor privies, of rosaries and public house raids, of love and marriage, of priests and religion, of scholars and schoolmasters.

This is a book that never palls or drags. It is boisterous and ribald and I am tempted to say that it is by far the funniest book I have ever read. It is also an accurate and revealing history of rural Ireland half a century ago and more. John M. Feehan writes beautifully throughout. I love this book.

John B. Keane

We live in a moment of history where change is so speeded up that we begin to see the present only when it is already disappearing.

R.D. Laing

Introduction

This book is a simple account of the lives of ordinary people in the countryside of half a century ago. I have recorded what I can remember about them before it all becomes a confused memory in the mists of the mind, a cloudy phantom of the past. I lived amongst them, shared their misfortunes, their sorrows and their scanty joys. I was so close to them that at times I even died their deaths. Our way of life took thousands of years to grow and develop and mature but it was destroyed in less than a generation and I was one of those who strangled it. I was a willing wheel in the machine of destruction that brought its beauty to an end. How that came about is part of this story.

There are few things as intriguing in old age as the renewal of the ties of one's youth, the resurrection of the undimmed beauty of a far-off childhood. This Irish countryside I love because I am part of it, part of the rain that lashes the hills, part of the wind that blows across the purple heather, part of the lowing cows and the singing birds. I have never really left it.

Sometimes I go back again and stroll reflectively through the fields, the lanes or the river bank and then a strange thing seems to happen. Almost at every turn I meet my younger self sprung from the earth full of amazement and wonder at the mysteries of nature, full of hopes and dreams of a world beyond the horizon, 'a laughing schoolboy without grief or care, riding the springy branches of an elm'. It seems to me then that we are all two completely different personalities held together by a fragile, gentle string. The youth believes he knows the answer to every question: the old man knows that life is a bewildering enigma and most of the time a closed book. Yet for both the green land of Ireland is alive and it is that which really binds them together.

9

I have gone to great pains and indeed used many geographical and historical devices to conceal the true identity of the enchanting countryside about which I write. It could be in any part of Ireland where I lived but I know that every reader of rural background will recognise in this book scenes he lived through as a child. I have changed the name and description of every person even though they are all long since dead. They are entitled to their anonymity as are the crumbling remains of their little homes that once rang with laughter and music and song. I grew up amongst them and we lived in the shadow of one another. In recording their story the honour is all mine and I hope to prove worthy of it. That old world is gone now and a great deal of the simplicity, joy and cheerfulness has been replaced by affluence, stress, strain and tension. But there is no turning back:

> *The moving finger writes; and having writ,*
> *Moves on: nor all your piety nor wit*
> *Shall lure it back to cancel half a line*
> *Nor all thy tears wash out a word of it.*

JMF

Our Village

The village lay partly in a valley and partly on the edge of an extensive windswept plain. To the south and to the west luxuriant wooded hills sheltered us from the great gales that surged in from the far-away ocean and at the same time gave refuge and protection to a rich, varied and abundant wild life. The song of the lark, the call of the pheasant, the bark of the fox were the very music, song and poetry of our lives.

To the north and to the east the great plain unfolded itself almost as far as the eye could see, broken only by a bog of purple heather, and clusters of tangled windswept trees, where ghosts glided by night and banshees wailed the cry of death.

People no longer believe in such things but in our village they were as real as the next-door neighbour, as real as the postman or policeman. They were not regarded as spirits of evil but as poor wandering confused souls who would not harm anyone if left alone. Indeed I never knew an old man or an old woman who had not at one time or another seen a ghost or heard a banshee. Some of them were known to be very friendly and Lahy the Liar often recalled how a banshee used to give him a drag on her pipe in return for a swig of poitín, which Lahy always carried around with him in a Lourdes water-bottle in case of emergency. "Tis how her throat got very dry from wailing the dead all the time,' Lahy said, 'and she liked to freshen it up with a little sup now and again'.

The cross-roads was the centre of our village, the axis round which our lives revolved. Here the men of the village, old and young, gathered in the fine evenings to hear the latest news, review the price of cattle, sheep or pigs, hold forth on political issues of the day and maybe close the evening with a game or two of penny pitch and toss. The men assembled at the cross-roads were not always a very mannerly lot. Almost every outsider who passed by was sure to be greeted with some derisive remark about his antecedents or native townland or indeed the odd unlucky one might get a belt of a sod flung by some anonymous hand in the crowd. It is not that individually the men were unruly but collectively they seemed to resent any intruder coming into or passing through our village.

But the cross-roads had other and more important implications for us. It was our lifeline to the great big world outside. The best of these roads, meandering and dusty, led to the railway station, where the two daily trains roused the village to wakefulness and from where hundreds of young men and girls, with their meagre belongings tied in a brown paper parcel, left their home forever to try to find a new hope in a far off land of dreams.

The same road led to the schoolhouse, where generations of barefooted, poorly-clad children learned to read, write, add, multiply, subtract and divide.

Ten miles further along this important road was the county town, the El Dorado of our childhood dreams. Here lived well-fed, rich prominent men, with a watch-and-chain in their waistcoats and a bowler hat on their bald heads. Here too lived beautiful, elegantly dressed women, so fragile and delicate that one wondered how the wind did not blow them away. They all lived in large magnificent houses with slates on the roof and a pump in the yard.

Tom the Turnip, so called on account of his balding head, was a council worker. It was his job to clear the drains and keep the ditches along this road clean, but Tom was always ready to rest on his shovel and have a chat with any passer-by, pronouncing solemnly on the affairs of the world and the foibles of human nature. 'The ladies and gents of the town, the quality, priests, nuns and Christian brothers,' he declaimed, 'don't have to relieve themselves at all. That's only for the likes of us. That's why God made plenty of grass in the countryside and none at all in the town'. I really believed Tom until one day I saw a Christian brother making use of the shelter of an old ruin in the graveyard after a funeral. Yet despite this evidence I was quite confused for a long time to come.

In all there were about fifteen houses in our village ranging from one-roomed thatched hovels to the slate-roofed abodes of the solid farmers. It used to be said that a respectable farmer had a son a priest or Christian brother, a daughter a nun, a pump in the yard, slates on his house, and the more irreverent added that he bulled his own cows – meaning, of course, that he owned a bull!

But most of the houses were small cottages, thatched with straw. These cottages usually had three apartments: a kitchen in the middle and a bedroom at either end. The boys slept in one room, the girls in another and the old couple on a settle-bed in the kitchen. The settle-bed was an institution in most Irish houses. It could be folded by day to make a seat or a bench and used as a bed at night. It was snug and comfortable near the fire. Its only drawback was its proximity to the turf which had the effect of attracting an unwelcome number of fleas.

There was, of course, no running water in any house. It had to be drawn from the village pump which seemed to have an inexhaustible supply. This pump only let us down once in my memory and that was when some poor demented unmarried mother had drowned her new-born baby in the well.

Some of the houses had an outdoor privy, a rough affair, well away at the end of the garden. It was usually painted green to blend in unobtrusively with the prevailing colour of the foliage. Others less fortunate trusted their anatomies to the mercies of hail, rain and snow, and the sparse shelter of a furze bush and they seemed none the worse for it all.

But those who had privies took a pride in them. They were always kept clean and the seats were scrubbed with coal-tar soap usually on Saturdays. Just inside the door there was a bucket of lime. A shovelful of this lime was put down the hole after one attended to one's needs and this had a very salutary effect on the lingering aromas. There were, however, those who liked to be up-to-date, to be more modern. They used top-soil in their privies because there was far more bacteria in the top-soil than in the lime and the said bacteria made short work of what was offered to them. Every Monday the weekly newspaper was cut up into suitable squares and stuck on a nail in a convenient place. Sometimes, however, it ran out and it was augmented by a copy of the *Irish Messenger* a religious magazine of piety published by the Jesuits every month. Apart from their hygienic uses these documents also provided useful reading materials during a sojourn, although it was at times infuriating to be reading an exciting news item only to find that the concluding part was missing – probably used by a previous customer. One Christian brother from the village freely admitted that the call to the higher religious life came to him while reading some spiritual article from the *Irish Messenger* during a happy sojourn in a privy.

Danny Molloy, a carpenter who specialised in the construction of coffins and privies and who was a recognised master of his craft, admitted that the best privy he ever constructed was a single holer he built for the canon in the days when he was young. He always praised the canon for maintaining it in a manner befitting its expert construction.

Inside the door was a little holy water font so that one could bless oneself before and after and collect a few indulgences at the same time. Pride of place on the main wall was an oleograph of Job sitting on the dung-hill with the caption: *The Lord giveth, the Lord Taketh away. Blessed be the name of the Lord.* On three walls outside most refreshing climber roses added a touch of colourful beauty to the establishment. The roses too served as a decoy, for when the canon took a stroll towards the establishment one never really knew whether he was going to prune the roses or attend to another urgent matter. Nevertheless he could sometimes be spotted in high summer reading his breviary or saying his rosary while sitting on the seat.

Of course privies had other uses for the more imaginative. One young farm lad learned to play the melodeon in a privy. Another always brought a deck of cards with him and played 'patience' during his free time. Old Kate always did her sewing and knitting in the privy and went through a serious emotional crisis when years later she moved to a new council house with a flush toilet. 'I never asked them council clerks for a pot for me arse in me old age!' she complained. But perhaps the most unusual use one of our privies was put to was that of a hardened bachelor who was doing a line with a servant girl for fourteen years. Every Wednesday and Sunday night they did their courting in the privy and if somebody wanted to use it they courteously vacated it and returned when the occupant had departed. Then with amazing suddenness they got married and a few months later a child was born. Evidently the damage was done in the privy and the theme of what went wrong was the subject of ribald comment at the cross-roads for many a long day.

In our village we all had different traits and characters, as different as the way we ran our lives. But there was one spectre common to all: that spectre was poverty. It was always there.

Money was a commodity talked of in awe and trepidation. To have money was the second most important goal in life, the first being to avoid going to hell. A labouring man earned twelve shillings a week and his food. I was a close friend of one such man, Johnny Joe. He was married with seven children. He paid one shilling a week rent for his council cottage. As well as his food the farmer he worked for allowed him to bring home a few pints of milk each evening. His wife, Biddy, took in washing from such single men as teachers and police. In the late spring and summer evenings he alternately planted his small patch of garden or cut turf for winter fuel. Johnny and his family lived on home-made bread, eggs, tea, rabbits, which were plentiful, blackbirds and thrushes, and for special occasions a salmon stolen from a rich man's river preserve, or a pheasant appropriated from the domain of the Great House.

I cannot say truthfully that the people of the village were really hungry but they had no luxuries whatever. They had to work ten hours a day, six days a week in order to even exist. This was the kind of harsh, pitiless exacting life led by thousands of labourers and their families throughout the country yet I have never known or heard of any one of them having to attend a psychiatrist or file a suit for divorce. There is surely a lesson here but what it is I don't exactly know.

The solid respectable farmer existed on a level only slightly higher than that of the wretched working man. Usually he had a somewhat bigger house with a spacious kitchen, a wainscotted parlour, two or three well proportioned homely bedrooms and a snug raftered loft.

Ornaments and decorations were few and far between. Most farmers' houses however had framed pictures of Robert Emmett, De Valera, the 1916 leaders and the Sacred Heart. But sometimes one came across rare gems of Meissen or old silver which had been looted from some gentleman's residence burned during the Troubles. Most houses also had a statue of St Jude, who was a great saint for getting husbands. A classic story told at firesides concerns a woman on her knees in front of St Jude praying desperately that a certain man would marry her. As she was praying this particular man's wedding party passed the door. In a fit of temper she threw the statue of St Jude out the window and it hit a passerby who was badly hurt. Remorsefully she brought him in and bandaged him. This led to a friendship which led to wedding bells. The first man turned out to be a waster and the lad who got the brunt of St Jude's statue turned out to be the perfect husband.

Inside the house the focal point was the open turf fire on the hearth, which burned continually night and day. It was on this fire that all the cooking, both for humans and animals, was done. The fire was at floor level and the constant bending up and down all day long gave the woman of the house that slim lithe figure so often commented upon by travel writers. It was also a contributing factor to the ease with which country women gave birth to their children.

The farmers' world, and therefore the world of the village, was governed by the seasons. It began in spring on 1 February, St Brigid's Day. The land had to be ploughed, harrowed and prepared for the crops. It had to be manured and the seed had to be sown: potatoes, turnips, mangolds, corn and whatever such crops each farmer chose to sow.

There was always an air of excitement about spring sowing as if the world was opening its womb to receive the gifts of man. We who were children endured a deep feeling of disappointment as we made our way unwillingly to school when the rising sun coaxed white steam from the earth, the ass-and-carts clucked their way to the untilled fields and birds began to sing their first songs of love. The grown-ups were gloriously free in a wild awakening world while we were chained to a musty school desk monotonously humming: two and two are four, two and three are five, two and four are six ...

And when the grown-ups sometimes told us that our school years were the best years of our lives we simply could not understand. We had a long road to travel before we found out that the good earth was a cruel and demanding earth as well. They too were chained to a different but harder task-master. Hour after hour, day after day, spring after spring they would till the earth and sow the seed with back-breaking monotony only to find at the end barely enough to keep body and soul together. For them the Lady Poverty held out no glorious vision. The vision was more likely to be a bed in a ward in the poor-house waiting for death.

When summer came the pattern of our lives changed again. The crops sown had to be attended to: the potatoes earthed, turnips and mangold thinned, the hay mown, turned and cocked. Perhaps most important of all was cutting and saving the turf so that our fires might burn brightly for the long cold winter ahead.

The long summer holidays from school left us free to help and I remember the great sense of pride that came over me when I cut my first bank of turf and turned my first field of hay. I was somebody at last.

Summertime too was the season of the great hurling matches and to us young boys it was a mere trifle to cycle ten or twenty miles, or even hitch a seat on a crossbar, to a Munster Final. Our heroes were men like Johnny Leahy, Lowry Maher, Seán Óg Murphy, Tull Considine and it was the ambition of every young lad to emulate them and wear the county colours one day. I remember once being asked by a school inspector which would I prefer: to be a famous film star or be a famous hurler. I did not hesitate in giving my answer. For me there was no greater fame in the world than to take the field for my native county.

Autumn came with its nostalgic colouring and brought with it one of the greatest events of the year, the threshing. The six o'clock whistle in the morning brought workers from the surrounding countryside to the threshing farm. They were voluntary workers who got no pay. When their turn came to thresh the same would happen and so for a day's work given a day's work would be returned. Occasionally during the day helpers would go around with a bucket of porter and give each worker a mugful to ease the parched throats dried by corn dust.

It was at one of these threshings I had my first drink. I was about ten years of age at the time and with my pal Jerry I stole a pint mug of porter when no one was looking. We proceeded at once to the quiet of the privy and there commenced our drinking. We were men at last. The stuff tasted horrible but neither of us pretended it was so. Very shortly Jerry turned green in the face as did I and we both threw up simultaneously. It was a salutary lesson that kept us sober at least for a few years.

When winter came with its long cold dark nights things quietened down in the village. It was a time for odd jobs, cleaning the ploughs and harness, repairing the fences that were broken and doing jobs of maintenance work preparing for the spring sowing.

But for those of us who were young then, the blazing turf fires around the hearth became the rostrum of the village where we listened in awe to bearded old men trace the momentous events of the wide world outside: events such as a drop in the price of pigs, a rise in the old age pensions, a death in the next parish, a goat that fell into a boghole, a man coming from a fair who saw a ghost, a woman who heard the banshee, or, this in a subdued tone, the latest murder committed by the hated British army.

In the winter evenings when I came home from school I turned the cows into the cowshed, milked two of them, cleaned out the shed and put down fresh straw for the night. After my own frugal supper I came to grips with my school exercises and rushed through them as quickly as possible. I was then free to go to a nearby farmer's house where old men gathered to discourse upon the world or to relate stories of 'old unhappy far-off things and battles long ago'.

At one end of the village under the shade of a large oak tree stood our local pub. The owner, Toss Ryan, farmed a few acres of land and between the land and the pub he was able to make a moderate living. Indeed there was little enough money lying around for drink and Toss depended largely on thirsty and loquacious travellers, known as 'bona fides', as well as the greatest boon of all, funerals.

Because our graveyard was the only one for many miles business was reasonably brisk. We had at least one, if not two, funerals every week. A funeral in rural Ireland was a social outing, a chance to get away from the drudgery of daily living, an occasion to thank God for being alive.

The mourners and the assembled guests, having buried the corpse decently and with due reverence, then turned to the more irreverent milieu of the pub where all and sundry drank to the eternal life of the deceased, it not being appropriate in the circumstances to drink to his good health. This pub sojourn was as much a part of the ritual of burial as was the Requiem Mass and indeed many's the man left a sum of money in his will to entertain his guests on the day of his funeral. Death was a very natural thing in our village. It was merely a transition from one state to another. It held no terrors so one might as well celebrate in a respectful manner and have a decent send-off.

The other kind of pub customer was what was known as the 'bona fide'. In those days the licensing laws permitted a pub to serve drinks up to midnight to 'bona fide' travellers who lived more than three miles away. The stupid legislators who concocted the law presumed that weary travellers journeying from one place to another were entitled to drink for two hours longer than anyone else. The reality of course was that men in one village got up on their bicycles and cycled to the next pub over the three mile limit. In fact it often happened that two parties of 'bona fides' going in opposite directions greeted each other half-way.

When midnight came it was sometimes difficult to persuade half-drunken farmers to go home. Toss' wife Molly ran the pub and although Molly did not press them too hard she had to keep a weather eye out for the police. In the event, however, of such a visit the following procedure was adopted: The bar itself was but a short counter at the end of the large kitchen. The moment the ominous knock came to the door all drink was cleared out into the back-kitchen. Molly put a statue of the Blessed Virgin on the table and lit a blessed candle in front of it. Then every drinker dropped to his knees and commenced saying the rosary. The police were then courteously admitted only to find a group of people at prayer. Over the mantelpiece and directly in the police line of vision was an allograph with the words: *Where two or three are gathered in my name I am also with them.* Molly would then invite them to join in a decade of the rosary and the unfortunate men, highly embarrassed, would make their retreat muttering apologies and regrets. After a discreet wait the drinks would appear again, the blessed candle quenched, and the rosary forgotten about.

Credence was lent to all this by the fact that Molly was an active member of the Children of Mary and in this capacity was noted for her work in promoting the family rosary. Molly was a deeply religious woman who at least outwardly retained the innocence of her girlhood. Although she was married to Toss she had never aspired to anything deeper in life than her daily routine of simple uncomplicated actions. She had all she wanted, a husband, a pub, her rosary, her novenas and it never occurred to her that life had any deeper meaning. She was a contented woman.

At the other end of the village was the shop – a delightful establishment which reminded one of a modern-day Aladdin's cave. It was run by Gladys, a virgin of undefinable years. She had a long graceful face that looked like delicately carved ivory, hair of silver, large blue eyes and carried herself with a grace and dignity that inspired both homage and affection. She was helped by her slightly deformed brother Dinny, regarded by many as a half simpleton, but who was no fool when it came to business matters. When the Redemptorists were preaching the mission in the village church it was usual for all, even back-sliders to go to confession and, so to speak, clean the slate. Dinny refused point blank to go to confession to either of the missioners. When asked why, he was as forthright as he was simple: 'Why should I go to them? They're strangers. I'll go to the curate. Ain't he a customer of ours?'

Almost everything needed by a small rural community could be had in Gladys' shop: food for man, animal or bird, shovels, spades, forks, implements and tools of all kinds, needles, thread, buttons, thimbles, mouth organs, tin whistles, jew's-harps, sweets, Peggy's leg, bull's eyes, liquorice. It was all there jumbled together and only Gladys and Dinny knew where each individual item was.

A smart-alec 'townie' who was passing through once asked Gladys for a condom. Without batting an eyelid Gladys said: 'Yes sir. What size?'

The flabbergasted smartie muttered: 'I don' really know ... I'm not sure ...'

'Well,' answered Gladys, 'come back when you do ... or if you like go down the road there to Danny Molloy the carpenter, who can measure you. He has a ruler marked in tenths of inches'.

Gladys was by nature a kind woman. She often took pity on young boys and girls who had no money and who longingly eyed her sweets. But she had one abiding obsession. She would never give charity. She gave gladly but it had to be earned. When she saw the yearning look in our eyes as we coveted her sweets she looked out over her rimless spectacles and told us that we could have a pennyworth if we cut a basketful of blocks, or swept the yard or drew turf to the kitchen or did whatever job she wanted done at the moment, And we were always willing to do it for the bull's eyes or Peggy's leg.

Her good nature extended not only to children but to adults as well. If someone ran into trouble through illness or some such mishap she would tide them over the difficult period with a little credit. If for some reason they eventually found it difficult to pay she applied her old rule of getting them to work off the debt by doing odd jobs. Many of these jobs were really unnecessary but it all resulted in her yard, her garden, her outhouses being the tidiest and most attractive in the village.

The other great centre of life in our village was the forge. It was always a very busy place with horses to be shod, wheels to be banded, farm implements to be repaired, gates to be made and a variety of other jobs which called for great skill and craftsmanship.

Black Tom, our village blacksmith, was the fifth generation of smiths in his family. He was a tall muscular man with a white flowing beard. This was unusual since blacksmiths did not normally grow beards for fear a stray spark might ignite them. There was also the problem of keeping the beard clean with so much soot permeating the forge. Tom's beard was mostly dull with the dirt except on Sunday mornings when he went to Mass. Then the beard was snow white and it was always my ambition to see how he washed it but I never succeeded. Neither did I ever find out whether he slept with his beard under the clothes or outside them.

But the forge had another use besides the shoeing of horses. It was a rural dentist's surgery and Tom was the dentist in residence. Sometimes he extracted teeth with a kind of pinchers he had for pulling nails out of horses hooves but this method was only used when the tooth was loose and rotten. The more normal method I experienced myself when I had my first tooth extracted. Believe me I have never forgotten it. Tom tied waxed hemp around my tooth with a special running knot. The other end of the hemp was tied to the anvil. Two men held me firmly with head upwards. Then the anvil was pushed off its block. The falling weight wrenched the tooth out with terrible pain. I was then brought into Tom's kitchen where his wife Maggie made me rinse out the cavity with lukewarm water and something called 'alum'. This was to stop the bleeding.

I have never forgotten that experience. I never neglected my dental hygiene in the years to come so much so that I was well in my fifties before I had occasion to visit a dentist again – this time a real one.

In his early years Tom had the reputation for roughness in his capacity as dentist. This tendency was cured once and for all when, as Tom caught the tooth with the pinchers, his patient grabbed a certain sensitive part of Tom's anatomy and whispered in his ear: 'Now Tom, we'll both be gentle with each other!'

On wet days Tom's forge came to life. Everyone with a horse to shoe or a car to mend came to the forge. On my way home from school I picked my way under a dozen horses to get to the farthest corner of the forge where I was given the special privilege of manually blowing the bellows.

Tom could neither read nor write but his speciality was mental arithmetic. He had at least a hundred customers who could pay him only when they sold the pig or threshed the corn which was usually once a year. Without the aid of pencil or paper he kept everyone's accounts accurately in his mind and when the day of settling came he knew to a penny what each one owed him.

There was great excitement in the village the day the first wireless came, but Tom was not unduly impressed. In those days it was not called wireless or radio. It had the more descriptive name of 'Listener-in'. Almost the entire village turned out to see the smart, clever men from the town put a large pole in a corner of the schoolmaster's garden and lead a wire from it to the chimney pot.

When everything had been connected we were all given turns with the earphones – there were no loud-speakers – to hear music, song, and a man talking in a far away place called Dublin. Tom listened in bewilderment and delight, although he had some reservations: "Twill bring no luck,' he exclaimed, 'for 'twill hole the skies and let more rain down'.

He was proven right. That summer was the wettest in living memory.

Our village was a very ordinary one. It had no great features of breathtaking scenery, no sea, no waterfall, no mountain. But there was a gentle beauty about it all – the green sensuousness of spring, the radiant and rich colours of summer, the gold and russet brown of autumn and the grey loveliness of winter. Nobody famous ever came from our village. None of its inhabitants ever achieved great public acclaim. We had no meteors flaming across the sky of life. We had only gently tumbling stars that together made for a thing of beauty.

The people of our village could be described in government statistics as unskilled. That would be a false description. They were all highly skilled, whether in constructing privies or making coffins, digging drains or cutting hedges, droving cattle or tending to stallions, thatching houses or making fences – even Lahy could boast of being the most skilled liar in the country.

I do not want to paint a picture of an idyllic village like Goldsmith's phony one. We had our sinners as well as our saints. Apart from Lahy we had four or five accomplished liars; we had idlers, petty thieves, rogues and rascals and indeed a flourishing crop of fornicators – but these came mainly from amongst the strong farmers from whom no servant girl was safe.

Yet despite this, or maybe because of it, there was a strong element of normality about our world and this normality generated a practical simplicity which contained within itself the elements of greatness.

But that world, my world, is gone. The village today has, in half a century, changed beyond recognition. It seems to me that it is in a stage of transition and it is neither one thing nor the other, or as Dan the Rat would more eloquently remark – 'It is like a mule's genitals – neither useful nor ornamental'.

Today every family in the village has not only a radio but a television also. There's only one thatched house left. All the others have been modernised and slated or replaced by grey-white bungalows. They all have electricity, running water and proper toilets. The privies are a relic of the past and for the most part have been demolished or covered with undergrowth. Multi-coloured baby-soft paper is used instead of the *Irish Messenger* and people seem to have no mind for a leisurely devotional read while attending to their little emergencies. But some few eccentrics refused point blank to use the new establishment. 'I have been giving my custom to the hedges and furze bushes for so long now that I couldn't change', one remarked.

The road to the town is now tarmaced, widened and strung with telephone wires. Motor-cars, lorries and juggernauts tear along it creating a deafening noise. Even the silence of the graveyard is disturbed. Recently one old man, whose family had been buried there for generations, requested that he be laid to rest elsewhere. 'I couldn't stick the noise,' he said, 'and to have to put up with it for all eternity would be worse than hell'.

Machines have now taken over and till the soil in an impersonal way. The freshness of the newly turned earth, the dignity of the horses, the scrape of the plough, the clean glitter of the furrow are all things of the past. The harvest too is mechanised to a degree where ten men were once employed one man is now enough. One good thing, however, is that the spectre of poverty I knew and experienced is gone. Everybody seems to have enough. Social welfare and dole has seen to that in such a way that it is now more profitable not to work than to work.

But all this is change which is an inevitable part of the law of life. When I was a boy the old people spoke of the momentous changes that took place during their lifetimes, and now that I am old I talk about the changes I have seen.

We cannot halt change. But we can accept it and use it to our advantage and perhaps find help and inspiration in the words of Cardinal Newman: 'To change is to grow; to be perfect is to have changed many times'.

LAUGHING VOICES OF OLD COMPANIONS

Full many a gem of purest ray serene
The dark unfathomed caves of ocean bear
Full many a flower is born to blush unseen
And waste its sweetness on the desert air.

Thomas Gray

Sometimes people ask me what were the influences surrounding my youthful days that ultimately led me to become a writer and a publisher. I think they expect me to say that I came from a literary background, that I grew up in the shadow of men of letters, that I devoured all the great classics of literature. The reality was very different. Although a literary milieu is laudable and to some extent necessary the only real teacher is life itself.

When Synge went to Paris to learn to become a writer Yeats made him return to Ireland, live among the poor and express them in literature. In London the publisher Jonathan Cape told Liam O'Flaherty to leave the city and go back to the Aran Islands. 'But there's nothing there except seagulls and fishermen', protested O'Flaherty.

'Well then write about seagulls and fishermen,' advised Cape.

Those factors which moulded my youth did not come from books or from literature. They came from the people, the great unwashed, the common herd, most of whom could not read or write. Like every village ours had its unique and matchless personalities as well as what one would call the normal people. These characters gave the village its flavour, its laughs, and sometimes its tears. In another setting and in more advantageous circumstances they would have been its great statesmen, great writers, great men of the world. But in the obscurity of our village they lived and died almost unknown.

Some mute inglorious Milton here may rest
Some Cromwell guiltless of his country's blood.

In this chapter I am going to introduce you to a few of them. I hope I succeed in bringing them to life for you. You are unlikely to come across their likes again. They are a lost generation that will never return.

The first of these great influences was Michael Lahy, known far and wide as Lahy the Liar. Indeed he himself was somewhat proud of this title. It seems to have run in the family as he had kinsmen known as Larry the Liar.

Once Lahy caught three salmon in waters that were strictly preserved. A stranger came along and asked him if he had any luck. Lahy proudly boasted of the three salmon. 'You obviously don't know who I am,' said the stranger. 'I am the new water-bailiff here.'

'Do you know who I am?' asked Lahy.

'No,' answered the water-bailiff. 'Well I'm Lahy, the biggest liar in Ireland. You couldn't believe a word I say,' was the smart reply as he quickly made his getaway.

Lahy was what one would call a spalpín, that is a wandering workman, and his speciality was cattle droving to fairs. Lahy slept in a loft over the cowshed in our yard. This concession he won in the following way: One beautiful summer's evening when I was about four or five years old I had been sent to bed early for some misdemeanour or other and in an act of bravado I managed to climb out on the top window-sill of our house. I lost my balance and fell headlong towards the ground. Lahy, who was just arriving, rushed forward, caught me and broke my fall. Had he not been there I could have been at worst killed or at best maimed for life.

My father never forgot this incident and some time later he gave Lahy the use of the small loft over the cowshed as his permanent base. The loft was reached by a ladder through a trap-door which Lahy kept securely locked. No one was ever permitted to enter this apartment. Once and once only I was let in for a look – but only from the top of the ladder. I have since been in the mansions of the great and the palaces of a dozen capitals but I never experienced anywhere the thrill of that one and only peep into Lahy's den. I thought I was looking into Aladdin's cave and I had been transported a thousand years back in time.

Every forbidden thing that a little boy could ask for was there: lamps, guns, fishing-rods, bicycle wheels, masks, pots, pans, footballs, mirrors, walking sticks, rabbit-traps, snares but Lahy would allow me to go no further than the trap-door. 'You are the only one I ever let look', he said. He neglected, however, to mention that everything there was 'borrowed'. Lahy never 'stole' anything. He had the best intention to return everything one day to its rightful owner. Sometimes, however, Lahy's restitution became a bit awkward.

The canon had a prize flock of turkeys and the bane of his life was the foxes. But it wasn't always the four-legged foxes who visited his pen. Shortly before Christmas Lahy helped himself to one of the canon's plump birds. He had a healthy fear of hell and he knew his sin would be forgiven only by making restitution and returning the turkey to its rightful owner – something he had no mind to do. However, Lahy found a way. He went to confession one Saturday night to the canon and confessed that he had stolen a fowl – he was careful to use the word 'fowl' and not be more specific.

'I will give the fowl as a present to you, canon,' confessed Lahy.

'Now my good man,' said the canon falling into the trap,

'that would not be right. To make proper restitution you should give the fowl back to its rightful owner.'

'Well, canon,' said Lahy, 'I offered the fowl to its rightful owner and he didn't take it.'

'In that case,' replied the canon, 'you are under no further moral obligation and you can keep the fowl.'

There was in Lahy strong traces of wanderlust which caused him to disappear, sometimes for weeks or even months at a time. Some strange force beckoned him on – that mysterious force so well voiced by Gerald Gould:

I know not where the white road runs nor what the blue hills are
But a man can have the Sun for a friend, and for his guide a Star
And there's no end of voyaging when once the voice is heard
For the river calls and the road calls and Oh! the call of the bird.

Whenever Lahy returned from his wanderings he adopted me and filled my head with stories, most of them wonderful lies:

'I was doing a bit of work for a gentleman near Dublin and we went to the races at the Curragh. The gentleman had a mare running in the last race and half way round the course I declare to God didn't the mare lie down and give birth to a foal, and in spite of that up she gets and gallops away and won the race. And what's more the foal came in second – we won a power of money that day!'

Lahy claimed he was once in England. He went there by foot and said that he walked across the Irish Sea because it was frozen over during the hard frost of 1918. When he came home he boasted how big the English farms were.

'I was on a farm there,' he said, 'an' 'twas so big that a labouring man would start out setting spuds in a drill and the drill was so long that by the time he got to the end of it he turned around and started digging and harvesting the finest crop of spuds you ever saw. And on the same farm they'd send out a young married couple to milk the cows and their children would bring home the milk'.

One bitter winter's day Lahy was complaining to his companions, Dan the Rat, Johnny Jump-up and Bill the Fool of how cold it was. Dan told him to shut up saying: 'What do you know about cold anyway? I remember when we was working in the six counties 'twas so cold that when we tried to talk the words turned into little lumps of ice and we had to boil the billy-can and pour the hot water on them so that we could find out what we were saying to one another.'

Lahy was not be outdone and quick as lighting he faced the challenge.

'You can talk all you like about the six counties,' he said, 'but no more that two miles from here I was gathering up a handful of sheep and the black frost was so bad that when a ram jumped off a big rock he was frozen in mid-air and he had to stay there for a week until the sun came out again and melted him.'

'But what about the law of gravity?' asked Dan, who had a little schooling. 'Did you never hear of that?'

There was just a moment's hesitation. 'Yerra, man alive,' quipped Lahy now in full steam, 'the frost was so bad that day that the law of gravity was frozen too.'

Lahy told me of a few brushes he had with the civil law. Once he said some fool of a civil servant called him up for jury service. Lahy had no mind to serve so he petitioned the judge who knew him well. 'Your honour,' he said, 'I beg to be excused. I owe a man £10 and he's leaving town in two hours time and I want to pay him before he leaves.'

'You're excused,' replied the judge. 'I don't want anyone on the jury who can tell lies like you.'

On another occasion he was up in court on some offence and he pleaded guilty. The judge ordered the jury to bring in a verdict of 'Guilty'. They retired and came back a few minutes later with a verdict of 'Not Guilty'.

'What do you mean?' said the judge. 'This man has pleaded "Guilty".'

'Well,' answered the foreman, 'we all know Lahy the Liar and no man would believe a word he said'.

'And by God,' said Lahy later telling the story, 'the judge had to acquit me'.

Lahy was truly my hero. To me his way of life was everything a child could desire. He lived by the principles that no man should trouble himself too much with the truth if he could get away with an exaggeration, nor should anyone buy anything if he could conveniently borrow it. He once heard a sermon in which the Devil was described as the 'father of lies'. This very much tickled his fancy and he subsequently maintained that the only way to overcome the Devil was to tell bigger and better lies than he could.

Once when we were lying at the back of a rick of turf I told him of my secret ambition to grow up and live like him. I was then seven years of age. He looked at me rather sadly and said: 'Don't be a fool, son. Stick to the learning and you'll get somewhere. You only see one side of my life – there is another. I'm only a tramp with nobody to care whether I'm sick or hungry, dead or alive. Often and again I wanted to give over my ways and settle down with a nice woman and a steady job. But just when I had myself talked into that a strange stirring would come into my blood and I'd have to be off to the river or the mountain or the fair, and then I'd think, what woman would put up with the likes of that – and so I never got round to it.'

The sun had set behind the hill, its last golden rays lingering on the horizon. There was a far-away misty look in his eyes. Then spoke softly and quietly: 'Here I am today, nothing but a vagabond, or like a tinker separated from his clan. No, son, stay with the books and the pens and the pencils – they are better instruments than the spade or shovel or the ash plant. Stay with the readin' and writin'. You'll go a long way in the world if you do.' And then with a twinkle in his eyes he said: 'Don't do as I do – just do as I tell you – and you'll be all right.'

One day while I was still a child Lahy died. It was Easter time and he had travelled to the town to make his annual confession. Just as he left the church he was struck by a newfangled motor car and by the time they got him to the hospital he was dead.

Danny Molloy worked all through the night to make a coffin for Lahy and the next morning Dan the Rat and Johnny Jump-up set off for town in a jennet and cart to collect the corpse from the morgue in the poor-house.

Lahy's body lay on a grey slab in the dead house, his clothes dishevelled, a piece of white calico covering his head. Dan raised one end of the cloth up and one could see Lahy's head covered in caked blood, his eyes and mouth wide open.

With the help of some paupers Lahy was lifted into the coffin which was tightly tacked down and placed on the dray cart. Johnny insisted on sitting up on the coffin just to make sure that nothing untoward befell Lahy. 'You could never trust the banshee,' confided Johnny in a whisper. 'She was great friends with Lahy and she might whip him out of the coffin in a split second and we might never see him again.'

Lahy's body was laid out in a barn swept clean and whitewashed for the occasion. A large kitchen table scrubbed white was his bier. Nell the Nurse washed him, closed his eyes with pennies, and put a small sod of turf under his chin to keep his mouth shut. The sod of turf was well concealed by his beard. Dan the Rat expressed the view that nothing on this earth could keep Lahy's mouth shut and from time to time he discreetly inspected it to see if by some miracle Lahy was not really dead.

He was dressed in a cast-off Chesterfield suit kindly donated by the canon and while he looked extraordinarily dignified in full pontificals there were those who thought that the top-hat reposing on his chest seemed a little out of place. Nevertheless the majority of our village held that where he was going a Chesterfield suit and top-hat consecrated by years of clerical wear could be a decided advantage.

From all parts of the county they came to pay their last respects to Lahy – tinkers, tramps, cattle drovers, farmers rich and poor. Even the squire himself in his knickerbockers accompanied by the judge turned up suitably attired wearing black arm-bands. A hasty collection provided funds for pipes, tobacco and snuff. Toss Ryan donated a half-barrel of porter for the thirsty who held up their mugs in Lahy's direction murmuring: 'May the Lord have mercy on your soul, Lahy, and on all the souls of the faithful departed'. To which the women, sitting round the walls of the barn, murmured: 'Amen'.

Six strong men shouldered his coffin and slowly walked at the head of a large crowd to the graveyard. The canon was indisposed and unable to attend so I went early to the open grave and filled a two pound sugar bag with fresh earth. I ran all the way to the canon's house with this. The old man, who was in bed, blessed it and later when they lowered Lahy into the grave I opened the sugar bag and sprinkled the blessed earth over the coffin. Then the crowd knelt down and the schoolmaster recited a decade of the rosary. Johnny Jump-up, Dan the Rat and Bill the Fool, his boon companions took off their coats and shovelled the earth until the grave was full. A couple of bottles of poitín were produced after the sergeant left and those who had missed the wake drank to Lahy's eternal rest. Then the crowd left in little groups telling and swapping some of Lahy's great stories. These wonderful stories have now been given permanence in a delightful paperback called *The Book of Great Irish Lies* by Myler Magrath.

A few weeks after Lahy's funeral the canon announced from the altar that Lahy's possessions would be put on display in the barn and if those from whom he 'borrowed' something could reasonably show it was theirs they could have it.

The display, presided over by the canon and the sergeant, looked like a kind of mini-market one used to see in the town on a fair-day. It was almost unbelievable that one human being could have accumulated such a collection. Yet they were an honest people and everyone claimed only what was his own. Lahy's soul had returned everything he 'borrowed'.

But his final secret came out when the schoolmaster found a small wooden box hidden under the straw in the loft. It contained hundreds of receipts for varying sums of money which over a period of forty years Lahy had donated to a religious order for the education of priests for the foreign missions.

When the canon heard about it he was flabbergasted. He shook his old wise head and half to himself murmured: 'Imagine that somewhere today amid the swamps of the White Man's Grave, in some leper colony, in the hovels of some primitive tribe dying of starvation, there are priests and nuns easing the misery and sufferings, angels of God, sent there by Lahy the Liar'.

Johnny Jump-up taught me the gentle art of 'poaching' which was of course nothing more than fishing illegally in preserved waters.

We spent the long summer evenings fishing and it was here I learned that Johnny was the greatest expert of all time. He taught me how to tickle a trout's belly under the bank of a river and then grab him by the gills; how to attract salmon by means of a small mirror attached to the line about a foot away from the hook. The salmon came out of curiosity to look at the mirror. Then he chucked the line and the salmon was hooked by the belly. It was all illegal of course but in another sense it was praiseworthy in so far as we were stealing the property of the English.

According to tradition Johnny got his nickname in the following way. One of the many competitive sports of those far-off days was the reaping race. A number of men, perhaps up to twenty, armed with scythes, would reap a field of corn, each to his own allotted section and whoever finished first was declared the winner. Johnny had won several such races in the past and had the reputation of being the fastest reaper in seven parishes.

A county final was being held in a field of corn just outside the town. There were six competitors of whom Johnny was the favourite. The atmosphere was tense with excitement. The bookies present had a busy day and the large crowd placed heavy bets.

Some few wags, anxious for a bit of devilment as well as the chance of making a quick buck, surreptitiously administered a strong purgative in Johnny's dinner.

The race had only just begun when the purgative began to work and Johnny felt an urgent call of nature. He squatted down and hid himself among the tall stalks of corn but of course he had slipped back a few yards behind the others. This happened a few times and by now the crowd, wise to what was amiss, began cheering. Each time Johnny went down the crowd shouted, 'Jump-up Johnny, Jump-up' and other ribald remarks. Matters were now looking serious and he had fallen quite a bit behind the others. But Johnny was not one to be easily intimidated. In a flash he whipped out his jack-knife and cut the entire backside out of his trousers. He was now able to answer all the calls of nature without squatting or ceasing to reap. Needless to say he won the race and won as well the nickname Johnny Jump-up. During the festivities that followed he managed to cover his behind with a yellow-meal bag 'borrowed' by Lahy but when the crowds had dispersed he prudently retraced his steps across the corn field and recovered the cut-away piece of his trousers and in no time it was stitched back into position.

June was Johnny's great fishing month. It was like a honeymoon to him when the wood-fly fishing season began.

'Don't you see,' he said as he introduced me to this fascinating art, 'early in June the flies on the trees gets a bit frolicsome and frisky and the male starts casting his eye around for a suitable female. Well anyway when contact is eventually made the two of them start a bit of you-know-what in the trees. After a spell they get so goddam crazy that they fall into the river where the big trout are waiting specially for them. Now let me tell you you should always study nature and if you do you'll never go wrong. Come along now and we'll start first catching the flies'.

He put me on the bar of his bicycle and we cycled along a leafy bohreen to a little grove at the edge of the river. It was high summer. Out of his fishing bag he produced a cigar box about nine inches square, and an ordinary bottle of transparent glass.

'You'll have to excuse me now,' he said. 'I have to knock off a bit'.

Bewildered though I was I was soon to find out what he was up to. He opened the cigar box and proceeded to defecate into it. When he was finished he half closed the lid and propped it up with a short length of stick. Seemingly from nowhere swarms of buzzing flies appeared and congregated on the object in the cigar box. After a few minutes Johnny tipped the stick and the lid closed trapping the flies. At one end of the box there was a hole and the flies began to make their way out. Johnny covered the hole with the opening in the bottle and steadily a stream of flies made their way out into it. When the bottle was about half full of flies Johnny corked it and put it back into his bag. He then washed and cleaned the cigar box and put it away until it would be required again.

We assembled our fishing rods and then Johnny let me into his great secret. He showed me how to put the flies on the hook.

'Have two flies,' he said. 'Put one on top of the other in the mating position and put them on the hook. Then float the line slowly down the river and the trout will think that the flies have fallen off the trees and they'll jump at them. In this way you'll get the best trout in the river. They must however be in the mating position. If they're not then the trout will think they're two queers or something and won't bite'.

Looking back I now think that must have been the best day's fishing in my life. After a few hours I had fourteen magnificent trout and Johnny had two dozen.

When I asked him if there was another way of catching the flies he explained: 'You could catch them with fresh horse manure,' he said, 'but it must be fresh. They're like ourselves – they don't want stale grub. Anyway you could not be going around after a horse all day with a cigar box under his tail. The way I showed you is the surest, best and quickest. But it doesn't always work. Sometimes the flies gets a bit moody and they likes a kind of a delicacy. I remember one time four of us went out fishing – the curate was with us – and we all knocked off a bit but the devil a fly came to us. After a little coaxing the curate agreed to have a go and I declare to my God but the finest swarm of flies ever came to him. 'Twas the good feedin' you know. The curate was used to good eatin' while the likes of us were living on tea, bread and red jam. The flies gets particular sometimes. Anyway what's wrong with the way I showed you? Some people might think what I set in front of the flies is disgusting. To us it is but to the flies 'tis paradise on earth. 'Tis all in the way you look at things'.

A profound philosophic principle I have never forgotten – beauty and ugliness are relative.

Johnny too was a renowned master of the art of cursing. Each curse was a gem in itself:

> 'May the lamb of God stir his hoof through the roof of heaven and kick you in the arse down to hell.'
> 'May you go stone blind so that you won't know your wife from a headstone.'
> 'May the devil cut your genitals out and feed them to the pigs.'
> 'May the devil throw you into the pit of ashes seven miles below hell.'

... and some few not very reverential:

> '... be the twenty-four balls of the twelve apostles.'
> '... my bicycle was hopping off the road like the curses of Jesus Christ off the windows of a whorehouse.'

Surely one can detect here 'some mute inglorious Milton', some Shakespeare gone awry.

Another of the village greats was old Danno. He was 90 years of age when I was twelve. He lived alone in a small two-roomed thatched cottage, spotlessly clean and tidy. He never married but, as he sometimes whimsically remarked, he 'was not entirely unfamiliar with the female parts'. He was quite philosophical about marriage. "Tis true,' he remarked, 'that a wife is always there when you want her – but on the other hand she's always there when you don't want her.'

Danno was a foundling, parents unknown. He spent the first twelve years of his life in an orphanage and was then apprenticed to a cobbler who taught him the art of shoe-making and shoe-repairing.

He was one of nature's gentlemen – one of those who gives you the feeling you've known him before you were born. His effortless conversation like a flowing stream made no demands on you. When he spoke he spoke out of friendship and not out of a desire to be heard.

Danno was highly intelligent. He learned to read, write and calculate at the orphanage and so was much better equipped to face the world than were most other boys of his age. He even learned how to serve mass and by watching the priest carefully when he carried his bag he also learned the rubrics of the last rites given to those about to die. Indeed there is a story told that once when the priest was on holidays a very simple peasant pleaded with Danno to give the last sacraments to his mother who was near death. Danno diplomatically declined by saying: 'I'm sorry I can't Joe, for the priest took his instruments away with him and 'twouldn't be right without them'.

He learned the old Celtic language and taught me how to count: Yan (1) tyan (2) tethera (3) methera (4) pinip (5) etc. He remembered some of the old religious knowledge questions before catechisms were printed: 'What is a bishop?'

'Holy man, well educated, consecrated and blessed by God above all the priests'.

He was a very prudent and careful man who put aside a

little every week for his old age and when he eased off in his seventies what he had saved, plus the few shillings old-age pension, enabled him to live in very frugal comfort.

Even though his earnings were small he managed to buy the occasional second-hand book and by the time I got friendly with him he had quite an impressive little collection of Irish books.

It was Danno who first introduced me to Irish fiction and Irish poetry. He loaned me the novels of Kickham, Pender, Sheehan, O'Hanrahan and many others and I found I could relate very much to these authors since they wrote about a world and a people I lived amongst and understood.

These books were fiercely nationalistic and in this they reflected Danno's own outlook. I have rarely ever met a man so strongly anti-British. Danno was a boy at the time of the Great Famine in which millions of Irish were deliberately starved to death in an attempt to decimate the Irish race. When I once questioned this he quoted the British economic adviser, Nassau, as saying words to the effect that if matters were not expedited only one million would die and that would not be nearly enough.

Sometimes, with tears in his eyes, he told me stories of what he saw himself: a woman with a child at her empty breast and three other children all screaming for food. The roads littered with dead bodies being devoured by dogs: a man carrying the almost naked body of his wife to be buried in some shallow grave accompanied by four crying children: a woman who crawled on her stomach about a mile to a small farmer's house and when they gave her a piece of bread she ate it so ravenously that she died on the floor.

Danno showed me the Famine mound in a field just outside the village where hundreds were buried, many not yet dead. In some of our walks together he showed me the remains of scores of ruined cabins from which whole families were evicted during the height of winter to starve to death.

But Danno's great delight was that he had his revenge on the British. During the land war he burned to the ground three of the mansions of the landlords who carried out the evictions and he personally shot, at varying times, twelve British soldiers and two Irish informers. So intense was his feeling that he sometimes said he regretted shooting them – he would have preferred to let them starve to death like the Famine victims.

He was tried for four of these but was acquitted for lack of evidence. It wasn't that there were no material witnesses but nobody would betray him despite offers of substantial rewards.

Danno's impact on me was to alert me at a very early age to the strong anti-British feeling that lies deep in the heart of every Irish man and woman. In the years that have passed since those days this would seem to have mellowed somewhat but I believe that is only on the surface. Deep down the brutality is not forgotten despite the most strenuous efforts by the revisionists to whitewash it.

His sense of wonderment at the changes he saw taking place during his lifetime was keen. He never condemned them, but like a child, marvelled at them. One day when he was in his ninetieth year he reminisced as we sat on the little wall outside his cottage. He had just come out of hospital where a tube had to be inserted to remedy a slight problem with his kidneys.

'I remember the first train,' he said, 'remember the first bicycle, the first motor-car, the first aeroplane, the first charabang, the first telegram, the first wireless. I never thought I'd live to see the first pissing machine.'

Danno died a peaceful death at the age of 95. Although a little weakened by rheumatism he kept his faculties to the end. Indeed for many years there was an apocryphal story going the rounds that on his death bed he was asked the ritual question by the administrating priest: 'Danno, do you forgive your enemies?' To which he replied: 'I have no enemies, father. I shot them all!'

For an old man with no known relatives his funeral was one of the biggest ever seen in the village. He would have been proud of the send-off he got. Even the army turned out to fire a volley over his grave. A lone bugler sounded the last post and then the reveille to call him to eternal life where he would await Gabriel's last trumpet call.

Probably closest to me of all was a lad of my own age called Timmy. His father was a tinker who mended pots, pans, churns and such objects. Every June they took to the roads and travelled the length and breadth of Ireland but in September they returned to their 'winter quarters' in our village. They camped in a snug opening in the wood, were sheltered from the prevailing winds, and from September until June, Timmy and his brothers and sisters attended the village school.

Timmy shared my desk and we became bosom friends. He taught me the great lore of tinkers and even some of their secret language called Cant, pronounced like the Irish word 'caint'. God was 'Dhaluin' and the mother of God was 'Naderum of Dhaluin'. A whore is a 'ripoch', 'beor' means pregnant, 'Iosport' an illegitimate child and 'Glocotes' the police. But they can be threatening too – 'If you blackguard me again be the Dhaluin seen rudil but I'll corib your jeel achust'. (By God almighty I will kill you tonight!)

Many long years later I had the honour of publishing one of our greatest Irish poets, Sigerson Clifford. In his book *Ballads of a Bogman* he has a poem about a tinker-boy with whom I could completely identify. Like my case the tinker-boy turned up for school welcomed by the pupils and master.

> *He bowed his head as the schoolhouse shook*
> *With the cheers of every one*
> *Then the master made me share my desk*
> *With the raggedy tinker's son.*
> *The days dragged by and he sat down there*
> *His brown eyes still afraid*
> *He heard the scholars' drowsy hum*
> *And turning to me he said ...*

'Now what would I want with X and Y
And I singing the crooked towns
Or showing a drunken farmer
The making of silver crowns?
'And will Euclid teach me to light a fire
Of green twigs in the rain,
Or how to twist a pheasant's neck
So it will not cry with pain?
'And what would I want with an ancient verse,
Or the meaning of Latin words
When all the poetry I'll ever need
Rings the throats of the singing birds?'

Timmy too approached the future in a very pragmatic way. He learned mathematics, or sums, so that he could add, subtract, divide and multiply. Irish he learned too because the tinker language was half Irish. Geography did not worry him much because most tinkers knew the roads of Ireland like the back of their hands. He loved history because as he said tinkers always love a good fight. Nature study was his speciality because all his life he would have to match his wit against rabbits, pheasants, hares, foxes and other wild life so it was as well to know as much as one could about their habits.

English was his bugbear. He saw no earthly use in learning it. His special dislike was the English essay. He could find no sense in writing reams of nonsense about a subject. Given an essay on 'Our House' he was short and terse. 'We have no house. We lives in two tents by the side of the road'. On the subject of 'Our Cat' he wrote: 'We have no cat 'cos very few mice visits tinkers. But we have two lurcher dogs for stealing hens and chickens'.

One day the master drew a map of the river Shannon on the blackboard showing all the principal features associated with our largest waterway. We were required to write three or four pages on this topic. To Timmy this was all so much rubbish and waste of time. He obediently wrote his essay

43

but it consisted of one sentence only. That sentence was a masterpiece of accuracy and brevity and said all that was to be said. The sentence was: 'There are water in the river Shannon'.

Timmy fully subscribed to a fundamental theological principle respected by all tinkers, e.g. a tinker could steal on a Friday without committing a sin. The basis for this principle was as old as Christianity itself. They believed that on the first Good Friday a tinker stole the six nails designated to nail Jesus Christ to the Cross thus lessening his pain very much and subsequently making it easier to take him down.

So Timmy confined his stealing to Fridays. I well remember the first time he showed me how to steal pheasants. We crept along close to the edge of the wood just before the birds emerged to feed. Timmy had helped himself to a fistful of raisins in the shop while Gladys was not looking. He threaded each raisin through with three or four long hairs from a horse's tail. Timmy then scattered the raisins near where the pheasants fed. As the pheasants picked up the raisins they could not swallow them with the long hairs and they began to scratch their necks to free themselves, entirely oblivious to their surroundings. At this point Timmy simply walked up and caught the bird. It was very simple and quick. Timmy then carefully collected the unused raisins in case a stray pheasant would eat them during the night. If that should happen the game-keeper would know there was poaching and would most likely keep a special eye on that corner of the wood.

Apart from the Good Friday aspect, stealing from the gentry was regarded as an honourable pursuit and in no way sinful. After all the owners were English whose ancestors had grabbed the land from the Irish and so long as they remained in possession they were fair game.

He was an expert pick-pocket too but he was careful enough to centre these activities on the town where he could get lost in the crowds. Drunken farmers who had wallets were easy prey but Timmy kept within bounds: 'Never steal too much,' he advised. 'A pound or two at a time is enough,' he said. 'Any more makes them suspicious. Never be too greedy. Never leave your customer short'.

He was also an expert locksmith. I have never known him to fail to get into a house, open a collection box in the church or a trunk waiting to be collected at a railway station.

Side by side we grew up together but I was the beneficiary. There was nothing I could teach him but he could teach me a lore and a way of life thousands of years old.

We left school and our ways drifted apart. As Sigerson Clifford so beautifully put it:

> *He went to the life of ribbon roads*
> *And the lore of the tinker bands;*
> *They chained my bones to an office stool*
> *And my soul to a clock's cold hands.*

Timmy became a scrap dealer, married and lived with his wife and children in his own tents. I lost contact with him and then quite accidentally I heard he was in a county poorhouse dying from the tinkers' disease T.B., caused by wettings and neglect. I called to see him and we had a long chat about old times. I asked him how was he for money and he told me with a knowing wink he was all right. Before he entered the hospital he made a pilgrimage to Knock Shrine and since it was to be his swan song he helped himself to more money than normal from the purses of pious ladies while they were singing hymns. 'I have a warm bed,' he said, 'plenty of food, enough money and am in the state of grace, what more could any man ask for?'

A few months later he died. The reverend mother of the poor-house rang me to say that he gave her a packet containing £200 to be given to me when he passed on. What should she do with it?

I thought quickly: 'Keep it,' I said, 'and give it to some special charity that you are interested in'.

She was profuse in her thanks. 'That's wonderful,' she

said, 'I will use it to send poor people on a pilgrimage to Knock Shrine'.

Did I hear Timmy's laughter in the clouds?

No. But I remembered an old Portuguese proverb: 'God writes straight with crooked lines'.

The village character in most villages is a thing of the past. As the years go by I notice a tendency to conformity. The individualist is a dying species.

But the big question is: What are we conforming to? Is it something better or is it something worse? Has advertising taken over? Are the hidden persuaders the rulers of our lives? Has the moron replaced the individualist? Has personal thought, however eccentric, made way for the empty chatter of plastic television personalities? Is it easier and more lucrative to go with the flow of the tide?

Lahy the Liar, Timmy the Tinker, Dan the Rat, Johnny Jump-up and a host of others are in their graves – graves for the most part unknown and unmarked. I cannot speak for the multitude but I can say that my world is all the poorer for their passing. But there is one shining truth. Rotting in their graves their skeletons are indistinguishable from the skeletons of the king, the queen, the pope, the president and all the quality who ran their world while they lived. Death is the great leveller. The justice of God cuts us all down to size and leaves us with a frightening sense of the awesome. But there is also His great mercy spoken by 'the writers of Revelation': God will wipe away all tears from their eyes; there will be no more death and no more mourning or sadness. The world of the past has gone.

LOVE AND MARRIAGE

If God made anything nicer than sex he sure kept it to himself.

Attributed to Red Kitty

In our village Red Kitty was reputed to be the principal dispenser of pleasure of the flesh, not only for the village itself but for the surrounding countryside. In a strongly Catholic community like ours this needs some explanation.

Love played hardly any role in the lives of the farmers and men of property. Marriage for them was based almost exclusively on property, land and inheritance. The sheer struggle for existence was the bonding which held most marriages together. Woman was seen as a mere provider of children and a somewhat upgraded domestic servant. Farmers' marriages were mostly arranged for a fee by professional matchmakers who took little account of the feelings of the couple.

There is a marvellous scene in John B. Keane's play *Sive* where Sive's guardian, Mike, timidly asks whether she should marry for love. The crafty old matchmaker, Thomasheen Seán Rua replies, directed at Mike's wife Mena: 'Will you listen to him! Love! In the name of God what do the likes of us know about love ... Did he ever give you a little rub behind the ear or run his fingers through your hair and tell you he would swim the Shannon for you? Did he ever sing the love-songs for you in the far-out part of the night when ye do be alone? He would sooner stick his snout in a plate of mate and cabbage or rub the back of a fattening pig than whisper a bit of fondness for you. Do he run to you when he come in from the bog and put his arms around you and give you a big smohawnach of a kiss and tell you the

47

length of the day was like the length of a million years while he was separated from you? Could you say that he ever brought you the token of a brooch or a bit of finery? ... Na! More likely a few pence worth o' musty sweets if the drink made him foolish of a fair day ... And to hear him blathering about love ...'

This powerful comment could have been written about almost any of the farmers in our village. The matchmaker usually won out in the end. Love played an infinitesmal role.

One such matchmaker from another part of the county gave me a detailed account of the procedure. It was equally applicable to our village: 'Suppose there was an ould couple with two sons,' he said. 'Well the eldest would get the farm and as soon as the ould couple got the pension they'd give a fistful of money to the next fellow so that he could get a woman and marry into her farm. He'd come to me then and I'd have to find a woman with a dacent bit of land. More than likely she'd have her father and mother livin' with her. I'd ramble up to them on a Sunday evening by way of no harm. We'd talk about the weather and politics and the price of pigs and anything else that would come into our minds. Mind you they'd know bloody well what I was there for. The girl would be all shy and red in the face and after a while she'd gather herself up into the room out of the way and then I'd tell the ould couple I had word of a match. Himself would want to know who the fellow was and how much he had. I'd mention a figure well below what we had in mind so as to give myself a bit of room for bargaining. If he was agreeable he'd say he'd want a lot more but we could talk about that later. Then the next Sunday, when the mother and daughter would be gone to second Mass, I'd call up with me bould bachelor and himself and meself and the girl's father would walk the land. We'd have to do that to satisfy my man that he wasn't getting a pig in a poke, and that the land was well fenced, and watered, with no ragworth, thistles or bouchalauns. We'd have a look at the outhouses and all the stock and make sure no stock were moved in from a neighbour just for the day. If my man was satisfied then I'd arrange with the girl's father to come another day by myself to talk about the arrangements. Man alive 'tis then the trouble would start and I might have to make several journeys before we'd finally fix on the sum of money the bachelor would bring with him. Anyway when we had all that fixed we'd name a day to go to town to draw up the writings. You see we'd have to go to a solicitor to put everything in writin'. You could never trust the word of a farmer, for he's so crooked that if he said the rosary with you he'd try to do you out of a decade. Anyway we'd all go to town, meself, the bachelor, the girl with her father and mother into a solicitor's office and everything would be put down on paper. The farm would be made over to the two when they married, the dowry would be lodged in the bank in the two names, the ould couple would have the right to be fed and to keep their pension, and they'd also have a right to one room in the house and a seat in the car to Mass on Sunday, and a whole lot of other things like that. Then they'd have to write their names on the piece of paper the solicitor would put in front of them and when that was over we'd go to an eatin' house for a feed of pig's head and cabbage and after that into the best pub in town for a bit of a celebration. We'd try to leave the couple alone so as they's get to know one another. At first they'd be very shy and he'd be lookin' at her like a cat studying a saucer of boiled milk. After a while they'd soften out and he'd start to call her by her first name and from there on they'd be no stoppin' the two of them'.

Most farmers' marriages were arranged in this way devoid of any finer emotions. Indeed this system lingered on well into the 1940s and was strongly supported by the church. Most Rev. Dr C. Lucey, late Bishop of Cork and professor of Social Ethics in Maynooth, usually began his lectures on marriage with the words: 'The only proper basis for Christian marriage is the mature deliberation of the parents of the parties concerned'.

A great deal of nonsense has been talked about the holy

sacrament of marriage in Ireland. If we look at its history we find that in ancient times it was pretty well a free-for-all. First of all the Church accepted *de facto* the concept of betrothal where a man and a woman agreed to live together for a year or two and if it worked out all right they could then uplift their relationship to the status of a Christian marriage.

The ancient Irish went even a step further and accepted concubinage as a normal way of living. In the fifteenth century one of the Maguires of Fermanagh had twenty-one children by eight different women, while an ancestor of Red Hugh O'Donnell had eighteen children by ten different women. If by any chance an Anglo-Irish bishop in one diocese prohibited concubinage the offending gentleman simply moved his entourage across the border to a diocese run by a Celtic bishop and there in some discreet inn he gambolled and frolicked to his heart's content.

Indeed it is recorded that his holiness the pope once offered an Irish prince, one Hugh O'Connor, the kingship of all Ireland if he gave up his fine concubines. It was a tempting offer but Hugh turned it down. Presumably he felt that the joys of five beautiful women in bed far outweighed a very shaky kingship.

But things had changed by the time I was growing up and concubinage was only a memory of the past. Nevertheless the role of women was not an easy one.

They were expected to be faithful to their husbands not out of any moral or emotional reasons, but because infidelity on the part of the woman could result in an offspring not entitled to inherit the farm. The cuckoo in the nest could not be tolerated.

Such restrictions did not apply to the male farmers themselves whose philanderings were not likely to affect the family inheritance. In this way their little deviations were not frowned upon. This was one reason why their wives tolerated infidelity in their men. But there was also another reason. Most farmers' love-making was bullish, crude and vulgar. It was learned in the farmyard, it smelt of the pig-sty and to a sensitive woman it was devastating. It was little wonder therefore that she welcomed a rest from his onslaughts and tolerated his meanderings. Here Kitty stepped into the breach. She herself openly boasted that she was performing a public service and indeed often claimed that she was responsible for keeping most marriages together and so protecting the inheritance for future generations. That she earned a little on the side was merely incidental.

Kitty was a tall, lithe, seductive woman with flaming red hair and laughing eyes. Her whole body seemed to be made for the joys of the flesh. She was a woman of amazing emotional agility. She sensed instinctively when a man was attracted by her and her fertile brain invented a hundred wiles to attract him further. She lived in a little cottage discreetly hidden from the main road. She made her living washing, ironing and starching collars. A farmer on his way to the creamery might drop in a bag of washing and perhaps if he had any spare cash in his pocket or felt a trifle love-hungry he might also linger a little longer than necessary. Indeed local gossip had it that even the squire occasionally honoured her with a touch of the most noble parts.

For a variety of reasons a few households availed of her laundry services in a different way and we were one of them. She came to our house every Saturday and did the washing there and in this way I came to know her well. She did our washing in the barn and my job was to draw the fresh water and empty the dirty water. We were often alone and from time to time she discussed the mysteries of sex. She talked freely about herself and she phrased her exploits in such sensitive and tasteful language that she might well be describing her First Communion.

I was about eleven years of age at the time and was astonishingly ignorant of the simple facts of life. The current theory amongst children of my age was that babies were found somewhere in the garden usually under the cabbage. I was shocked beyond belief once when Tom the Turnip told me that one day when he was cutting a head of cabbage he accidentally cut the backside off a baby. From then on I handled the vegetables in our garden with the greatest of care.

Kitty soon put an end to these childish illusions. In a matter of fact but reverent way she explained how babies really came into the world. She then opened my trousers and had a look. I suppose that at eleven years of age she was not impressed with what she saw. She only remarked: 'You're too young yet for the fireworks. Come back in four or five years and things will be more exciting'.

That was how I learned the facts of life and everything seemed sensible since I was daily watching cows, bulls, dogs, bitches, cocks and hens and a variety of other species but it was a bit of a shock to realise that I had been a fool for so long.

Only once before did I ever have a suspicion that everything was not what it seemed to be. One day I heard Lahy the Liar telling a group at the cross-roads that on one of his travels he peeped in over the wall of a nudist colony and he was very disappointed because he was unable to tell who were the men and who were the women because they had no clothes on! When I asked him what a nudist was he told me to get to hell home as such things were not for youngsters.

Did I go back to Kitty when I was sixteen? You'd love to know, wouldn't you? Well you can stay guessing! Suffice to say, however, that many years later she married a man from far off parts. Whether it was the prowess of her husband or her new philosophy of life, she was faithful to him, much to the discomfort and disappointment of the farmers. She reared a fine family who did well for themselves in the world, and about ten years ago Kitty died a happy and holy death fortified by the full rites of Holy Church.

At her funeral most of her past customers turned out suitably dressed for such a memorable occasion, all showing a decorous respectable amount of grief. It was an extraordinary scene – a mixture of prayer, liturgy, sorrow, nods, nudges, winks and ribald remarks as to the probable outcome of Kitty's encounter with St Peter at the golden gates. The general consensus of opinion was that, even if her credentials were not fully in order, she'd get in anyhow since Peter could never refuse an invitation from a beautiful woman to show her the outstanding sights of Heaven especially the well stocked celestial hay-barns.

Of course it happens to everybody at some time in life and I know of no more exhilarating experience than the sensation of first love. I was about twelve years of age when it happened to me and she was just twelve too. Her name was Nuala. In appearance Nuala was like a delicate portrait painted by Gainsborough – slightly reddish hair which seemed to colour her skin with a mysterious hue that glowed particularly in the soft lights of evening. Her eyes mirrored a strange ethereal tranquillity which could only have been the reflection of her guileless soul.

We sat side by side in class and an unknown affinity floated between us. Sometimes when the master punished me until I cried the tears welled up in her eyes too. I used to seek her out on my way to and from school, but especially during recreation time when all the pupils played games and I could touch her hand or her hair in a game of 'tig'.

On the way home from school I tried to be near her without letting the others see what must have been obvious. Strolling barefoot along the dusty road with the scent of lilac in the air it was magic to be alive and near her. Sometimes, I picked her a little bunch of forget-me-nots, her favourite flower. Other times I climbed a crab tree or slipped into some farmer's orchard to steal a sweet rosy apple for her.

One day on the way home from school we got separated from the others, not entirely accidentally. We turned down a leafy lane that led to the bog. The hawthorn bushes, arched over our heads, were bursting like foam in some garden of Eden. Bunches of primroses and violets lay like bouquets on the lush green grass. Except for the orchestra of birds singing all around us everything was silent. We sat down by a little stile and I made two daisy chains – one for around her neck and the other as a crown for her head. 'Now you are my queen', I said. In that moment I owned the whole world and felt a joy not of this earth.

As I placed the crown of daisies on her hair I drew closer. Her face turned up towards me and my hands mysteriously entwined her head. I gently guided her lips towards mine and kissed her with tenderness. The world seemed to whirl around me. I was at one with her that beautiful summer day, intoxicated by the smell of the flowers, soothed by the sound of the humming bees, the chirping of grasshoppers and the call of a distant cuckoo.

There was always something about that first kiss that lingered on in my memory. It shone like a gem of 'purest ray serene' in the dark cavern of life. It was wonderful to be alive. I was twelve and in love. We looked deep into each others eyes for a fleeting moment and then she said, 'Let's go home'.

Shortly after that I left the village and lost contact with Nuala. The fairy light of first love had fizzled out and she later married a friend of mine. Unlike most rural marriages it was a marriage of love and a happy one.

By one of these strange turns of life as I was writing this chapter Nuala died. I went to her funeral on that beautiful summer's day without a cloud in the sky. Wreaths of flowers were everywhere on and around her coffin. And once again I remembered, as I looked into the cruel open grave, that other beautiful summer's day more than half a century before, when I kissed her and crowned her my queen.

In such a terrible moment of life words simply do not come. There is only a walled up emotion inside which language is powerless to convey except in the words of a poet:

Alas that Spring should vanish with the rose
That Youth's sweet scented manuscript should close

The Nightingale that in the branches sang
Ah, whence, and whither flows again, who knows!

If the marriages of my youthful days were such humdrum and crude affairs how come that they worked out so satisfactorily in the end? Given their basic ingredients one would have expected them all to be disasters.

I think that the answer to that question lies in the extraordinary fatalistic philosophy of the peasant – not only in Ireland but all over the world. Put simply it is this: *They expected nothing from marriage and when they got a little they were delighted and thankful. In the case of the love-match they expected everything and when they did not get it they were frustrated and miserable.*

The harsh struggle for existence also helped to keep marriages together. Unlike the better-off they had no time to be 'hungry for the nameless' – because they were hungry for their daily bread. Bit by bit as they built their lives together they achieved some small degree of success and these little rays of sunshine brought them some comfort in their struggle to live. They accepted their lot in life and saw in it the will of their divine creator.

In our village too we had the occasional unusual love affair or marriage. One such was a small farmer who was courting a girl for fourteen years and eventually after some pressure from her parents and from the canon he named the day.

As they stood together before the altar the canon asked him the usual question: 'Do you take Josie to be your lawful wedded wife?' There was a slight hesitation and then he murmured 'Yes' and promptly dropped dead! The canon with great presence of mind, sensing future legal and inheritance problems, pronounced them man and wife and then administered the last sacraments.

A few years ago when I seriously began to collect material for this book I visited the homes of many of the older people of the village. I did this not just to jog their recollections of the past but to refresh my own failing memory. One such person I visited was Nell the Nurse.

In those days the doctor lived far away in the town and it was only in the most serious of cases was he ever called. The ordinary run of illnesses, colds, 'flus, measles, mumps, births and deaths were capably handled by Nell. She had no formal training as a nurse but her trade was passed on to her by her mother and so on for three or four generations back.

I knew if I could get Nell to talk I had a good chance of unearthing some of the secrets of the village. But I was disappointed. Nell was the soul of discretion. Beyond remarking that 'there were more fathers in the parish than husbands' she kept her silence.

But she did tell me one unusual story, well worth recording here. At this time she was in her late eighties and bedridden. She made me place my hand on the Sacred Heart picture over her bed and swear that I would never write it until she was dead. I did this with due solemnity and then she told me her story. Since she is now many years dead I am free to write it.

'You remember,' she said, 'Madge and Sarah Curtin who lived in a little cottage far into the bog.' I remembered them well. Often when I was cutting the turf I slipped into their cottage to boil the kettle for a drop of tea. Sarah was a dressmaker who was an expert at converting cast-off clothing into wearable apparel. She was all day busy at her machine. Madge cultivated the garden, tended the flowers, looked after the hens, geese and turkeys and generally kept house. When I first knew them, at the age of 14 or so, they were in their late fifties.

'Long years after you left the village,' Nell continued, 'Sarah died. I washed her corpse, laid it out in the coffin and after the wake they brought it on a dray car to the graveyard for burial. It was a fine respectable funeral.

'About three months later Madge died too. She died of no known sickness – she just pined away with a broken heart after Sarah and one morning some lads going to the bog found her sitting in her rocking chair, a rosary twisted through her fingers, dead.'

Nell paused for a moment and then said, 'Swear again on the Sacred Heart for what I have to say might frighten you.'

I did as she asked and she continued: 'Well I washed Madge and laid her out, and found out she was not a woman at all – *she was a man.*

'Luckily there was no one in the dead-room at the time so I kept my silence and Madge was buried alongside Sarah as two devoted sisters should be.

'Well of course I was curious and I knew that they originally came to the village at the turn of the century from a place about sixty miles away. I had relations in that part of the country and bit by bit over the years I put their story together without ever letting out the truth.

'Sarah was a dressmaker married to a small farmer. She met Madge, whose real name was Joe, and who was of course a man, and they fell in love. Joe was a gardener and he was married too. One Christmas time they disappeared and local gossip had it that they eloped together to England. Of course they did not. They turned up here as two sisters and bought a little cottage in the bog near the village. You must remember that 60 miles in those days were the same as 600 miles today. Nobody would ever think of looking for them as two sisters in a far-away bog.

'I have kept my secret until now,' she continued. 'When I am dead you can write it.' She then resumed her silence and would say no more.

When I left Nell's cottage that day I was in a kind of a daze. It was one of those dull autumn days, warm and sultry. Suddenly I was overcome by a powerful but inexplicable desire to visit once again their cottage which I had last visited more than half-a-century before. I drove down the old bohereen, now tarred and smooth. At the end I parked the car and walked across the bog to the little cluster of bushes where once their homestead stood. All was in ruins. Only the scattered remnants of the walls remained. Nettles and briars covered what was once the kitchen floor. A rat darted from the gaping sooty hole that was the fireplace. The desolation suited my mood.

What secrets lay behind those ruins? What kind of a life did they live together? I know from my childhood that they said the rosary every night. They went to Mass in their ass and cart every Sunday. They never missed a mission. What happened afterwards? What did they talk about in those long winter nights that spanned nearly half-a-century. What a powerful theme for a novel! Only the ruined walls know the answers to these questions and these too are crumbling into obscurity and oblivion and bringing with them the deep secrets of Madge and Sarah. That is as it should be and is only right. Together they now rest in peace. They may have broken the laws of church and state but they kept most faithfully the law of God: *The mark by which all men will know you for my disciples is the love you bear one another.*

Pat Muldoon was a strong farmer with sixty acres of good land and a fine house with slated roof. He lived with his father, a quiet unassuming man, and his mother who was a rather bossy type and ran their lives with a firm hand. She emphatically refused to let Pat marry because as she said, 'No two women are going to rule my house'. So Pat dragged his life along until his mother died. He was then in his late fifties. He immediately went to the matchmaker to find him a suitable companion.

While the matchmaker was casting his net around Pat made a novena to St Jude to help, and he also included in his prayers a petition to cure a large wart growing on his navel.

Whether it was St Jude or not the matchmaker came up with a sound sensible proposition. In the next parish there lived a small farmer with two daughters – one was a youthful twenty-eight who looked twenty-one. The other was an old thirty-five and looked forty-five. They were both available and, according to the father, each had a good dowry.

Without hesitation Pat picked the younger one and so

the wedding was arranged for the following Shrove Tuesday.

Pat bought a new navy-blue suit, a new shirt and tie, new boots and a pair of yellow gloves and duly turned up at the altar on the appointed day with his best man and friends.

Unfortunately, however, a little mishap took place the day before the wedding unknown to Pat. The young bride-to-be was in love with a local carpenter and they eloped to England together. The old farmer was in a bit of a puzzle but as he was a man of common sense and enterprise he put on his thinking cap and on the morning of the wedding he turned up at the chapel with the older daughter dressed up in a hastily put together wedding dress.

He boldly walked her up the aisle to her place at the wedding prie-dieu. When Pat looked and saw it was the wrong woman he almost panicked. But a lifetime of subservience to his mother helped him to accept the situation obediently and he went through with the ceremony.

In the chapel yard afterwards he upbraided the farmer and pointed out with some feeling that he had been tricked.

'Indeed you have not been tricked,' the farmer stated emphatically. 'That young bitch ran away with a penniless carpenter yesterday. What was I to do? I couldn't leave you standing waiting in the church. You'd be the laughing stock of the county. So I did the next best thing. I brought along her sister. Anyway you have no cause to complain. She has the same dowry; she can bake, milk and feed pigs and calves and is a better housekeeper than the other one. And I can promise you she'll be up early and she'll be between two buckets of milk in the cowshed every morning at seven o'clock before you're awake. Isn't that what you want a wife for. Surely you don't think you're Rudolf Valentino?'

Pat, in his simple way saw the sense of the argument and he accepted the situation. In those days the idea of going away for a honeymoon had not yet caught on. The happy couple and their guests adjourned to their home where all ate and drank and caroused for the day.

Pat wasn't entirely sure of his duties on the wedding night so he sought the advice of his best man, Bill Daly. Bill was a bachelor who felt he was not expert enough in these matters to give advice so he put Pat on to Tom the Tinker who was supplying the music and who fathered fourteen children himself. Towards evening Pat and Tom were seen in earnest conversation over a few whiskeys and it is reasonable to assume that Tom gave generously of his expertise. It was later rumoured that Pat was worried about his age and his head of grey hair. The tinker reassured him by saying: 'Don't mind your grey hair. There's many the mountain with snow on the top and heat in the valley.'

Later that night when all had gone home, Pat, his aged father and his new wife knelt down in the kitchen to say the rosary. When it was over herself went up to the room to bed. Tom and his father sat in silence staring into the fire smoking their pipes and spitting on the floor. After more than an hour the father suggested to Pat that he might care to go to bed.

'How can I go,' asked Pat sharply, 'when that one is above in me bed?'

The old man explained to Pat that things were changed from the old days and instead of sleeping with the sheep, dog and the goat he was now expected to sleep with his wife. Pat slowly made his way towards the room remarking: 'I've lived all me life in this house and all I can say is, whenever a contrary or awkward job had to be done 'twas always me that had to do it'.

Years later I visited Pat. He had five lovely children and herself was expecting the sixth and the head of grey hair was as unruly and wild as ever. If time had not melted the snow on the mountain top neither had it cooled the heat in the valley.

The marriages of the poor were based rather on love than on material gain. Because they had no dowry they could not afford a matchmaker. I have known young couples who were so poor that they could not afford a ring.

They depended on the goodwill of Black Tom who curved a horse nail for them at the forge. One day I met a friend of mine and his young bride coming from the church after his wedding. They sat together in a borrowed ass and cart which held their entire possessions: a few bags of straw for a bed, a collection of empty flour bags as sheets, and rough discarded sugar sacks as blankets, a small collection of pots and pans, a bag of turf and the clothes on their backs. They were moving into a tiny cottage at a rent of a shilling a week to begin together the greatest adventure of life. If love could survive these conditions it could survive anything – and most mysterious of all, love did survive.

But change has crept up here too and that world lives only in the memories of my generation. The matchmakers are no more. More sophisticated methods have replaced them. The young women of today are well briefed through the media in the subtle act of stalking a man and landing him. But at least their relationship is based on affection and compatibility if not on romantic love. Rightly so, women no longer tolerate their use as objects, as servants, as walking incubators. They are free at last and the quality of life is all the better for this.

If Red Kitty were alive now her prospects would be fairly dim. Pre-marital sex is the norm and it would not be too hard to count the number of virgins over sixteen in most villages.

Courting is no longer done in hay barns or on the sheltering side of a ditch. The young couples now besport themselves in the back of luxury cars or disappear to another town for frivolous weekends.

The spectre of poverty has also disappeared and even the poorest couple has running water, electricity, cookers and fridges. That is as it should be. There is nothing wrong with innovational change. What may well be wrong is the way we handle it.

RELIGION

The religion of one age is the literary entertainment of the next.

Emerson

Religion in our village was a very practical affair. It reflected life on the land. It was a case of sowing and reaping, buying and selling. 'As a man sows so shall he reap' was an old proverb applied to the land. It was also applicable to our religion. As we were taught the man who prepared his soul and tended his seed in this world would reap a good harvest in the next.

For us everything was made simple. We did not understand the subtleties of theology. We believed that God came on earth, established a church, which provided the seeds and the fertilisers in the form of rules and commandments. All we had to do was to cultivate and husband. That church was represented by the priests and we were in duty bound to obey them for they spoke for God.

To a large extent our attitude towards the priests had a deep-rooted historical origin. During the centuries of British oppression and brutality the only voice the common people had was that of the priests. They were educated men who spoke out for their flock and defended their rights. Unfortunately that ended with the founding of Maynooth College by the British. The church did a complete u-turn and gradually became a powerful instrument of imperial policy. Nevertheless the long-standing and deep respect for the clergy died hard and as I grew up they were still held in awe and respect, even though the crumbling of their power and influence had begun.

The God they put before us was an old man like Brian Boru or John O'Leary the Fenian. He sat on a golden throne surrounded by angels playing harps. He was a severe man of justice, who had an endless army of clerks counting up all our failings, *even every idle word men shall speak,* all our sins, and for these he would mete out the most terrible punishment.

We were expected to run our lives by the Penny Catechism. This catechism reminded us of how depraved we were – because Adam and Eve took a bite of an apple – *our whole nature was corrupted. It darkened our understanding, weakened our will, and left in us a strong inclination to evil.* We were also severely warned against reading the stars in a newspaper, having our fortune told by a tinker-woman at the races, or believing that if a hen came into the kitchen with a straw on her tail it was a sign that a visitor could be expected. *It is also forbidden to give credit to fortune-telling, incantations, charms, spells. All superstitions, observance of omens and accidents are also very sinful.* Under the pain of grievous sin I was commanded *to pray for kings, and all in high station* – and that included the hated king of England and the local landlord. It also taught us that *it is sinful to resist or combine against the established authorities or to speak with contempt or disrespect of those who rule over us* – and that meant the British rulers.

To come to more personal matters, we were warned against *all immodest songs, discourses, novels, comedies and plays and against all immodest looks, words or actions and everything that is contrary to chastity.* To bring home to our sinful natures how we should shun such occasions we were urged to beware of *lascivious looks or touches, idleness, bad company, all excesses in eating and drinking and whatever intends to inflame the passions.*

To tell a jocose lie was also sinful: *No lie, jocose or otherwise can be lawful or innocent and no motives can excuse a lie, because a lie is always bad and sinful in itself.* Obviously Lahy had somehow or another missed that one!

The penalties which our God handed out were severe. There was a general judgment where we would be put on trial for any of the foregoing grievous sins and God would say to us: *Depart from me you cursed into everlasting fire which was prepared for the devil and his angels.* Then we would spend the rest of eternity tormented in hell.

Yes, our God was a strange severe man. He loved pain and expected us to seek it out and 'offer it up'. He kept a rule book handy and judged accordingly, even though the rules were written by frustrated clerics in Rome. He condemned all human love expressed sexually and had no feel for the anguish and torments of human beings. For him purity was more important than love. He regarded war and killing as good provided it advanced the course of the church. He preferred the rich and powerful to the poor and his servants demonstrated it at every turn. In short he was a God devoid of all human feeling – a creation of ascetic theologians.

Yet some basic God-given instinct in us told us that such a God did not exist and this was a lot of crap but we had to live with it outwardly and tolerate those prophets of doom who toadied to the clergy. They moved around among us like candlesticks in a dead-house. They lived miserable gloomy lives and tried to make us do likewise.

However frightened I was I took some consolation from the fact that when I got to hell all my friends – Lahy the Liar, Dan the Rat, Tom the Turnip and all the others would be there to keep me company. Dan had a theory that the next world was like the Great House with an Upstairs and Downstairs. All those who lived by the catechism would be upstairs dressed in long mournful clothes, sitting around in armchairs listening to polite music. The rest of us would be downstairs carousing, card playing and telling yarns. Despite the fear I did not find it too hard to make my choice.

The canon ruled our village with an iron fist in a velvet glove. He felt personally responsible for the salvation of each and every one of us. He firmly believed that on the day of general judgment he would have to answer to God for each one of his flock and so he was determined to wallop us into heaven one way or another whether we liked it or not.

Like so many priests of the time his great blind spot was

sex. Sins of the flesh in his eyes spelt only one thing – the royal road to hell, and he was determined to keep us off that road.

Indeed he took practical action here. He actually strolled along the more out-of-the-way roads after dark and did not hesitate to use his blackthorn stick to drive the courting couples from their little love-nests on the sheltered side of a ditch. The couples of course got the hang of this and discreetly slipped into the fields, in hay-cocks or convenient hay-barns. This perplexed him somewhat since he could no longer find them although he knew by certain sounds they were there. He frustratedly remarked once to a colleague: 'Isn't it a terrible thing that I cannot go for a peaceful walk along a quiet road at dark without having to hear all those sinful couples and they grunting with passion'.

His sermons on sex were thunderous affairs. Fire, brimstone, hell, damnation awaited the sexual sinners. There was no hope whatever for them. They suffered especially in those organs with which they sinned which took the form of an embarrassing enlargement and extension. This led one frolicsome farmer to make an arrangement with Jack the Cow Doctor to cut out the offending instrument after he died so that he would not have it in hell. This he did after a remark by Lahy the Liar that he would require a trailer in the next world to carry it around with him.

Second only in entertainment value to his sermons on sex came his sermons on money. In those days there was no such thing as computerised giving. Everyone gave what they could afford towards the support of the priests. Collections were taken up at the church twice yearly, at Christmas and Easter and the list of contributors were read out off the altar the following Sunday.

As he read these lists the canon was unable to resist a running commentary. He passed over the first dozen or so whose contributions were in the 'pounds'. It was when he came to the shillings the fireworks began: 'Jack Ryan seven and sixpence. Now Jack was at the races a few weeks ago and I bet you he spent more than seven and six there.

'Joe Murphy six shillings. I saw Joe staggering drunk around the town on Christmas Eve. How much did he spend then?

'Tom Carty five shillings. Tom has a fine well-stocked farm yet all he can afford to give me is five shillings. No wonder he can't get a wife if he's so mean.'

And so it went on and on to the delight of the congregation. No one was offended. Indeed the whole performance was such a farce that it was regarded with some pride to be 'mentioned in dispatches'.

Only once was deep offence taken when the canon had the 'flu and he cut the proceedings short by simply saying: 'I have the 'flu today and I don't feel able to read out the lists. Suffice it to say that everyone in the parish paid their dues except the sergeant and Lahy the Liar'.

The sergeant was deeply hurt at this remark. It was not so much his failure to pay since everyone knew it was an unfortunate oversight. It was the fact that he was coupled with his old adversary, Lahy the Liar.

The curate, on the other hand, took a softer view of life. He divided sins into two categories. Firstly there were sins of selfishness and he saw most of these sins as grievous. Secondly there were sins of jollification which he saw as relatively harmless. He could not subscribe to the view that a fellow should have to suffer eternal torments all because he got too enthusiastically involved with a pair of pretty legs. But he was ruthless in his approach to selfishness. Most of our actions, ethical as they appeared outwardly, were based on strong deep-rooted selfish motives and a lot of this expressed itself in cruelty towards our neighbours or indeed our nearest kin. Years later he told me that his most painful memory of the parish resulted from a casual conversation he had with a middle-aged married woman. She had been twelve years married to a well-to-do farmer and had four children. He was civil enough to her for the first year of her marriage but after that he took a turn against her and for eleven years refused to speak a single word to her. In that period of time they had three children and it can only be left to the imagination how that was achieved as well as the indignation the poor wife had to suffer.

The curate was so appalled by this that the following Sunday he preached a fiery sermon on love, kindness and tolerance in marriage. He elaborated on his sermon by saying: 'I know of one couple where the husband has not spoken to his wife for several years even though they had children. That man is nothing more than a brute and a pig and if any crime calls to heaven for justice this one does'.

The real sting in this story came during the next few weeks. The curate told me that in that time more than thirty different men came up to him and said: 'Was it me you were referring to in your sermon?'

In other words he thought there was only once case in the parish. It now transpired there were over thirty and this was probably only the tip of the iceberg.

Most of these men were products of their time. They were brought up to believe that women were only chattels, breeding and working machines, who had no rights other than to do what they were told. Nevertheless an explanation of this kind does not take away from the terrible psychological pain suffered by generations of Irish women.

Even though the canon was one of the old school who saw women in that role, nevertheless he was a very good priest and the kindliest of men. While he condemned the sin of sex he showed great mercy to the sinner. Again and again he put his hand deep into his pocket and gave substantial financial support to unmarried mothers until they were able to adjust to life again. He treated them with courtesy and graciousness unlike so many other priests whose sole desire was to get these women out of the parish as quickly as possible.

One of the great religious events in my life as a boy was The Stations. In order to augment their meagre income a little more the clergy selected a house in each townland where once a year they would hear confessions, say mass and make a small collection. My great joy in this event was that I was very often chosen to be the altar boy and to serve the mass, and that meant I was one of the elite allowed to sit at the breakfast table with the owner of the house, the canon, the postman, the sergeant and other high dignitaries.

For at least a month before the big day the farmer and his wife would be busy preparing the house. The outside would have to be whitewashed and the inside painted. Tables, chairs and floors would be scrubbed, presses cleaned, cobwebs taken from behind the pictures, and any little defect in the furniture repaired.

The privy got special attention. It was newly painted inside and outside, a fresh lot of pages from the *Irish Messenger* would be put on the nail on the wall. Jeyes fluid was liberally sprayed in every nook and corner and the old bucket of lime replaced. In some of the more devout families a crucifix would be hung on the back of the door just for the day.

As an added precaution, however, the women of the house would take out of storage an important implement known as the canon's pot. This was a special deluxe bed chamber pot reserved solely for the clergy and put to use only when the weather was too inclement to make the trip to the bottom of the garden. This pot was set on a low stool in the middle of the floor in the best upstairs room. On each side a blessed candle was lit, no doubt to give it the proper liturgical setting. The canon could therefore be sure of a correct devotional attitude right through his visit.

All the locals, men and women, would turn up dressed in their Sunday best, go to confession, attend mass and leave a modest contribution in a closed envelope on the makeshift altar.

It was a social occasion as well as a religious one and everyone, especially the women, displayed themselves to their very best. When the breakfast was over the priest gathered up his instruments and drove away in his pony and trap. Then the fun would start. From somewhere a mouth-organ or melodeon would appear and the dancing would start. The man of the house would produce a barrel of porter and distribute it liberally amongst the men, while the women would be treated to lemonade or ginger wine. As the day wore along many of the younger couples would disappear into various parts of the outhouses or hay barn while their elders sang themselves hoarse dribbling porter from their lips. The diversion would end only when the drink ran out and then everybody went home to sleep it off. Some of the men, however, found their way to the pub and spent the rest of the day carousing and celebrating their new-found spiritual insights.

The two other great events in our lives were First Communion and Confirmation. I well remember both these days. I was seven years of age at the time of my First Communion. The evening before Tom the Turnip cut my hair with a horse machine and left only a small fringe in front. I then had my first bath – or at least the first one I can remember. I got into a big tub of lukewarm water and scrubbed myself from head to toe. We had all been to confession that day and had spiritually cleansed ourselves. Many years later the curate told me that first confession day was one of the high points in a priest's life. Not because of any religious high but because of the sheer fun of listening to the children's sins. Of course at that age we did not know what a sin was so we confessed anything we felt guilty about: robbing orchards, stealing sweets, cursing, pissing bad words in the snow, forgetting our morning prayers – the list of absurdities was endless.

It had been drummed into us that this was the happiest day of our lives but sad to say it left me unimpressed. The only high I experienced that day was that I accumulated about four shillings in pence given to me by generous adults and I spent the most of it with Moll the Babber who had set up a dray cart with sweets, fruit and all sorts of delectable eatables. The concept of God swelling in my soul was far beyond me.

Confirmation came some years later. Again it had been impressed upon me that a great change would come about in my life on that day. The Holy Ghost would descend upon me and I would receive his gifts. They were Wisdom, Understanding, Counsel, Fortitude, Knowledge, Piety and Fear of the Lord. Unfortunately they passed me by. I concentrated more on the small cash gifts given to me by kind adults but this time I spent the money on cigarettes and availed of every opportunity to hide behind a headstone in a corner of the church to have a quiet smoke.

Since Confirmation took place only once every three years there were about a hundred pupils crowded into the little church. The bishop went around through the pews and in a kindly way asked each of us a simple question from the catechism which we could hardly miss. The only one that faltered was Ned the Gander who was not over-burdened with brains. The bishop asked him why was Easter time so important for Catholics. At first the Gander was puzzled but then it seems as if a light from the Holy Ghost struck him. His face brightened up and he answered: 'My Lord, 'tis important for us all because it is the time of the two day races at Limerick Junction!'

The other great event in our village was the mission. Every few years, usually in summer, two religious order priests descended upon us and each evening for a whole week harangued us towards the royal road to heaven. The priests were either Redemptorists or Capuchins – once the Franciscans were very popular but our own priests noticed a tendency on their part to show an unusual interest in attending to the needs of sick parishioners who had the name of having a good strong bank account. When such parishioners died there was usually a clause in the will leaving a sizeable sum to the Franciscan Order. Their services were quietly dropped and other religious orders used instead. In an indiscreet moment the canon was heard to say: 'I have no intention of adding to the wealth of the rich sons of the poor St Francis!'

The mission lasted two weeks – one week for the men and one week for the women. It was considered injudicious to mix them seeing as how there were different names to certain sins.

The ceremonies started each evening at eight o'clock with Rosary, Benediction, Sermon and Confessions. The highlight of the evening was of course the sermon. The preaching was worked to a plan. The first night the sermon was on Death, the second night on Judgment, the third night on Hell. Then when the congregation were truly terrorised came two nights on the scarlet sins, namely the sins of sex – and a final night's preaching on some local sin as advised by the canon, such as making poitín or stealing turf, drinking or working on a Sunday.

The sermon on Death was frightening. The most vivid descriptions were given on the agonies of death – indeed I remember one preacher who gave an actual performance of the death throes of a sinner. He did it so effectively, even to frothing at the mouth, that he fell backwards out of the pulpit and nearly died himself.

Judgment was vividly described – the countless millions of people in the valley of Josephat all queuing up to be judged. Stewards trying to cope with major problems, such as sanitation, for it was necessary even in death to keep men and women apart. The unfortunate souls were judged with amazing rapidity and dispatched with haste to the broad wide road that led to hell. Only the odd one was seen making his way along the road to heaven.

The descriptions of Hell were also frightening – devils shovelling hot coals on top of people – beatings, torture of the most excruciating kind. Indeed one such sermon affected Tom the Turnip so much that he could stick it no longer. He rushed out to the pub to drown his terror and was later in the evening arrested for drunk and disorderly conduct and for staggering around shouting on the top of his voice: 'Up God and fuck the devil!'

The church was always crowded for the sermon on the

scarlet sins. People from far-away parishes came to titillate themselves on the morsels of erotica dropped by the missioner. He was usually fairly lurid in detail – the sinful sheets which would be hanging in front of us with our names written on them as we entered the hall of Judgment; the extended organs which might conceivably cause a traffic jam; all the children not born because of wasted semen would come alive and flail us – all this rubbish and much more too crude to mention was flung at the congregation. But some strange inbuilt peasant common sense told them that all this was again just plain crap and they finally viewed it as an interlude of pornographic entertainment.

One good thing about the mission was that its appeal was entirely emotional. After a week or ten days everything was forgotten and slowly but steadily the people dropped back into their old ways and old habits as if nothing had happened. Our mission was remembered only as one more piece of entertainment in our drab cruel world.

Death in our village was also a major religious event although strange as it may seem the people had a rather fatalistic approach to it. It was just one more great event in our lives which had to be gone through with and one might as well make the best of it.

When somebody died Nell the Nurse took over and, maybe with a helper, washed and laid out the corpse for the wake. Nell was careful and meticulous in her duties. So well did she do her work that you wouldn't know whether the final product was going to the grave or on a holiday. From time to time she let her close friends into her secrets: 'First of all you must scrub down the corpse well and above all block up the openings in the lower part of the body, and in the case of a man you must tie up the top of his engine with a bit of waxed hemp. This is most important in case there would be any sudden commotion in these parts that would be the cause of vulgar noises coming from the coffin during Mass. Putty is the best for this because it hardens although you could use a bit of plaster of paris as well. You must try to make the corpse look as well as possible so that the relatives will say "God bless him, doesn't he look the picture of health". You can do this by using a little yella meal as powder – dab it lightly all over the face. And if you want a little rosy colouring you could dampen the corner of the *Irish Messenger* and rub it lightly to the cheeks. Again if there are any teeth missing you could fill in the openings with putty. By doing all this you can make the corpse look as if he were going to a wedding instead of to a graveyard'.

When Nell was finished with the corpse it was waked in the principal room in the house. Most people in the village would like to pay their respects so they turned up at one time or another during the night. It was unlucky to go to the wake alone – one should always go with one or two others.

At the moment of death the clock on the wall would be stopped so that everyone who came in could see the time of death. Lighted candles were put around the corpse and a dish of snuff laid nearby. Everyone who came in knelt down, said a few prayers and took a pinch of snuff and said, 'The Lord have mercy on the dead'.

Everything had to be treated with great respect. I remember once getting the father-and-mother of a clout on the jaw from the woman of the house because I lit a cigarette off one of the blessed candles. Any snuff that was left over was put into the coffin so that the corpse would not be short in the next world. It was also usual for some relative of the dead person to wear his or her clothes on the day of the burial. It was believed that if this were not done the dead person would have no clothes in the next world.

In our village the funeral was a great social event. Unless it was a young person or someone who was killed accidentally, there was no real sorrow. But there were important customs to be observed and any failure to do so could cause great offence.

The coffin was taken directly from the house to the graveyard – it is only recently the custom of bringing the body to the church the evening before has crept in. If the graveyard were nearby the coffin was carried on the shoulders of 6 strong men. If it were some miles off a hearse was hired, but when the hearse came to within half a mile of the graveyard it was stopped, the coffin taken out and carried the remainder of the way.

It was an old belief in our village that the last person buried in the graveyard would have to act as servant to all the others until the next funeral, and I once saw most unseemly behaviour when two funerals arrived at the same time. There was a rush to get to the graveyard first and this involved abusive language and fisticuffs unworthy of a funeral.

Digging the grave was also an important task entrusted only to friends. No grave was dug on a Monday unless a sod had been cut off it the previous day. It was also important that the correct grave be dug, since in those days only the few had headstones. I have seen rows in our graveyard and families coming to blows over where the body should be buried. When they were digging the grave of one well-to-do farmer they found the remains of a two year old child a few feet below the surface. Since the farmer had no such death in the family many ribald remarks were passed as to the parentage of the child. However, the explanation was much simpler. It was the body of a tinker-child whose family had no grave and who buried their infant in a respectable grave at the dead of night. The remains were reverently re-buried in another part of the graveyard.

I remember one old farmer who was buried in one graveyard only after a long dispute. Each night after his burial his family could hear the clanking of chains from the haggard. After a week or so of this unnerving noise they came to the conclusion that not only was he buried in the wrong grave, but also in the wrong graveyard. In the dead of night the relations raised the coffin and brought him to another graveyard some miles away. The clanking of chains stopped forthwith.

People were normally buried in their family graves but

there was one exception to that rule. Bachelors usually had graves to themselves. They were not buried in the same graves as women even though the women were relations. It was felt that the rules of decorum should always be observed and no undue temptation should be put in anybody's way, even in the grave.

When the corpse was buried and the priest had left the graveyard refreshments were produced. It was considered an insult if one did not partake of at least one drink. Sometimes this too got out of hand and old scores were settled in a non-peaceful way. I remember one such funeral fracas which had its origins in alleged land-grabbing. At the end of the day four had to be brought to hospital, and ten others were treated by Nell the Nurse.

We were not however shamed by such things. Our religion was a very practical affair. It had little to do with God or goodness. It was simply another dimension to the struggle for survival. We tried as best we could to avoid the few big sins but we conveniently forgot the multiplicity of small ones – but as Lahy once remarked: 'Sure if God has any spark of common sense he'll understand'.

But all that has changed too. Our God today is no longer the God of rules and regulations. No longer the avenging God trying to catch us out in a moment of weakness. He is a God of infinite love and understanding.

The young priests today preach an entirely different God to the one we knew. God is our friend, our life's companion who understands and tolerates human weakness. He is someone we can turn to in trouble or in joy and someone who lends a helping hand along the road of life.

The old thundering sermons on death, hell and sex are all gone but I have to admit that I miss them. They were great fun and provided us with much entertainment.

Computerised planned giving has replaced the biannual collection and we are no longer treated to the lists of subscribers with running commentary.

Even death has changed. Nell the Nurse is long dead

and gone. She has been replaced by funeral parlours in the local towns, where the corpse 'lies in repose'. There are no more saucers of snuff or pipes of tobacco as these would be out of place in the refined atmosphere of the modern parlour.

This strange new God takes getting used to but for us all the old one dies slowly. Probably the hardest thing for my generation is to undo the past and unlearn what we were taught. Yet despite the beauty of this new God of love I sometimes miss the stern old warrior with his rule book and his voice like thunder and his fierce punishments. But change is overtaking us rapidly and there is no going back now. As I have remarked before it is what we make out of the change that counts – not the change itself.

PATRIOTS AND POLITICIANS

I slept in a kind of a trundle bed in my parents' room. Danny Coffey made it out of a discarded coffin that was being made for a child who was expected to die but who subsequently recovered. He removed all religious signs from it, put two rockers – one at either end – and made it as snug as the bed of a prince. Although in later years my school companions riled me about being raised in a coffin I did not find that this fact had any inhibiting influence on the course of my subsequent life.

One of my earliest memories is that of waking up in the morning, peeping out over the edge of my coffin, and seeing three or maybe four men asleep in the large bed and perhaps two or more on make-shift pallets on the floor. Leaning against the wall were several rifles.

These men were the IRA. They were on the run from the British soldiers, particularly from the hated Black-and-Tans who were the equivalent of the German Gestapo of later years. Our house was a safe house and different groups came regularly in the darkness for a meal and a night's sleep. After a breakfast at dawn they would be gone again for it was unsafe to stay very long in any one place.

I was born into this generation – the generation that finally routed the British from part of our country after hundreds of years of oppression. But it would be wrong to assume that the people of our village were great patriots. They were not. Indeed I subsequently heard the IRA complaining that it was with the utmost difficulty they found one man in the village to watch the police station and report on the comings and goings

Hundreds of years of indescribable brutality, equalled

only in history by Stalin and Hitler, had beaten and crushed our people into subjection, had turned them into slaves, and worse still, they came to like their slavery and to accept it as their norm. I remember years later the schoolmaster telling me that during the week after the 1916 Rising he discussed it with about fifty people. Only one had a good word to say about it – and that would have been about the percentage throughout the whole country. Seen in this light Pearse's idea of a blood sacrifice to awaken the people was very sound. Yet when it did happen the percentage jumped to only about 20% still leaving a strong 80% who preferred their chains. With few exceptions the people of our village were happy to wallow in slavery and subjection. They had become so demoralised that they were little more than rational morons.

Later on however, in the 1918 election, the Republican candidates swept the boards. But this had nothing to do with an awakened sense of patriotism. What happened was that the British threatened to introduce conscription into Ireland, and to save their own skins they voted Republican. This 1918 election is much quoted today by yuppie historians as giving a mandate to the IRA to make war on the British. It gave no such a thing. It was simply an anti-conscription vote and not an anti-British or pro-Irish one. With the exception of a few thousand idealists who were prepared to sacrifice their lives the vast bulk of the population remained respectful and obedient to their British masters. The IRA never got a mandate from the Irish people. They fought the British against the wishes of the Irish people, as they are still doing today.

I grew up listening to the sound of rifle fire, tip-toeing across ruined bridges, watching cottages being burned to the ground and sometimes having to look at young man being kicked and beaten around the roads by the Black-and Tans. My worst experience was seeing a family friend tied to the back of a Crossley tender and dragged behind it. By the time they reached the town he was dead. To make certain however they mutilated his body with bayonet stabs. It isn't easy to forget these things and even harder still to forgive, and when I listen to yuppie politicians today telling me that I should honour and respect those Black-and-Tans I cannot help wishing that they had witnessed some of the scenes I did as a child. I do note however that none of these yuppie historians or politicians are willing to give up the massive pensions and salaries they enjoy as a result of the freedom the IRA won for them.

The gauleiter in our village was the squire. He owned thousands of acres of land for which he charged high rents to farmers. He and his family lived in luxury in an imposing mansion which dominated the whole countryside. They were British settlers who were given grants of land plundered from the Irish. They were British to the core. They did not recognise any separate Irish identity. To them Ireland was merely another English shire.

Yet in many ways the old squire was a kind man. He regularly visited his older tenants when they were sick, arranged for them to go to hospital, very often at his own expense. He had a deep interest in all local happenings and supported local sporting activities and teams with his own money.

One of the great annual events at the Big House was the celebration of the king's birthday. Gentry from neighbouring big houses came with their frilly bejewelled ladies to drink the king's health and formally send him felicitations. In order to promote the established order of things the squire invited well-to-do farmers whose table manners could be depended upon to this function and almost all accepted. The master's son, known for his wild and unruly conduct, caused a sensation when he asked one of these farmers returning from the function how his tongue was. The puzzled farmer did not understand. He said there was nothing wrong with his tongue. 'I'm glad to hear that,' was the caustic reply. 'I thought it might be out of joint from arse-licking!'

The squire's wife, the Lady of the Manor, was a great horsewoman, so much so that her facial features became more and more horse-like with the passing of time. She never missed the Dublin Horse Show and for those days her face reached an ecstatic brilliance that at times was hard to distinguish from what was on display.

It was when she was returning from the Horse Show that she had an encounter with Lahy the Liar which is still talked about in local folklore. It seems that Lahy had been drinking in the pub and as usual ran short of money. Five fellow drinkers offered Lahy a pint of porter per man if he greeted and kissed her Ladyship as she got off the train. Nothing daunted they moved to the station. A coach and four was waiting for her Ladyship with its complement of flunkeys and lackeys. When the train drew in and stopped the porters and flunkeys rushed to open the door of the carriage for her Ladyship. As she alighted Lahy moved swiftly, threw his arm about her, and kissed her, saying: 'Wisha, welcome home Moll Cooney'. Now Moll Cooney's name was coupled with Lahy's for many a year and it was a tribute to his cunning how he used it to advantage on this occasion. Lahy was forcibly removed by the flunkeys but he quickly made his way back to the pub with the five others and claimed his five free pints.

Now Lahy was always a man capable of exploiting every situation to its fullest and the following day he called up to the Great House to apologise. His Lordship, who knew Lahy well, opened the door and said: 'Well Lahy what do you want?'

'Your Honour, Sir Lordship, I came to apologise for what happened at the station yesterday. I had a few drinks taken and I mistook her Ladyship for me ould friend Moll Cooney, and I disgraced myself.'

'Ah forget about that Lahy,' said his Lordship, who was not without a sense of humour. 'Come in and have a quick one.'

Lahy went in, took off his old battered hat and left it on the hall stand. His Lordship gave him two glasses of whiskey and on his way out Lahy was astute enough to take his

Lordship's hat off the hall stand instead of his own.

This gave him an excuse to come back the following day to return the hat 'mistakenly' taken, knowing full well that his Lordship would not wear the hat after Lahy. That was exactly how it happened. His Lordship told Lahy to keep the hat and as well he gave him two more glasses of whiskey. So the final result of Lahy's kiss was five pints, four glasses of whiskey, and a new hat!

The squire and his family were truly British although they always claimed they were Irish. When the Second World War broke out his two sons joined the British army at once, despite appeals from Irish leaders to join the Irish army. One of them was killed and the other returned safely home. The Great House was effectively run by a housekeeper of a high degree of competence and this allowed the squire and his lady to travel abroad most of their lives. This housekeeper had a young daughter who grew into a very beautiful girl and long after the old couple were dead the remaining son took a deep interest in the young daughter. She was well educated, intelligent and attractive. It was a real love match and they became engaged. The girl's mother opposed the match strongly on the grounds that they came from different backgrounds, and a different social class, and the marriage simply would not work. But the young couple were too much in love and they ignored her advice.

One morning, a week before the wedding, they left the house together for a stroll in the demesne woods. The son brought along his gun in case, he said, they met a pheasant on the way. Late in the afternoon their bodies were found in a spinney. They had died of gunshot wounds.

As far as one could piece the story together when the mother failed to stop the marriage, she revealed to them the truth – that the girl was the squire's daughter by her – they were brother and sister. Calmly they made a suicide pact and carried it out in the wood. Shortly after that the mother went insane and died in a mental home.

With no heir the great estate was sold off and it is now

back in Irish hands again. The only trace of the squire and all his glory are his family's sad neglected graves in the local Protestant graveyard.

At the time when I was growing up in the village the days of the Anglo-Irish gentry were slowly drawing to a close. The Treaty had given us a large measure of freedom – what Michael Collins described as the 'Freedom to become free' and in our internal affairs we had almost complete control.

But Collins' successors abandoned his goal of a 32 county Republic and settled for membership of the British Commonwealth. But all the country did not go along with that view. A sizeable proportion followed De Valera and his Fianna Fáil party. They inherited the mantle of Pearse and the ideal of 1916.

The Fine Gael government imposed an oppressive regime and jailed large numbers of Republicans. It was the old British method of brutality which had never succeeded, yet our new government were too blind to see that.

Eventually De Valera and Fianna Fáil came to power and a wild euphoria swept through the country. Bit by bit he began to dismantle our connection with Britain in spite of a terrible economic war, in spite of the almost total opposition of the Church and in spite of the fact that Fine Gael backed Britain to a man. Fianna Fáil was seen as a great national movement and not just a political party. How some of the next generation of Fianna Fáil betrayed every ideal of its founders and, consumed by greed, became even more British than Fine Gael does not concern this book, but in those days Fianna Fáil and Ireland were synonymous.

The politicians of those days were men of the highest integrity. They were men of their word and they saw their roles as representing the people in the fullest sense of the word. They were badly paid and they had no perks or pensions.

One such politician was our local TD whom we shall call Thady. He was a large strongly built man with a walrus moustache and a ruddy jovial countenance. He was every-body's friend and it did not matter what political party one belonged to he treated them all as human beings.

On matters not strictly political the schoolmaster usually composed his speeches, which he learned off by heart. Once when a memorial to a local writer of the nineteenth century was being unveiled he learned the short speech by heart. At the unveiling he marched across the platform bravely and began: 'Very Reverend and Reverend Fathers, ladies and gentlemen'. Something must have snapped inside of him for he couldn't remember the next sentence. He paused and coughed, and the schoolmaster sensing what was wrong, elbowed his way towards the platform. Thady began again:

'Very Reverend and Reverend Fathers, ladies and gentlemen', but the words would not come. He made a third attempt and failed. Just then a voice from the back shouted 'He have an air-lock!' and the crowd dissolved into riotous laughter.

By the time the laughter was over the schoolmaster had given him the cue and unabashed he started off in full swing. It was a rousing speech and he ended it by declaring: 'If the young people of Ireland keep to the spirit of our great writers of the past a shoneen will be as rare as a red Indian in Manhattan'. The crowd burst into loud applause, but the heckler at the back had to have his say: 'Where's Manhattan, Thady?' he shouted.

Thady lost his temper. 'How in the name of Christ do I know,' he roared. 'Don't I have enough on my mind besides that bullshit'. He sat down amidst the wild cheering of the crowd.

Another time he showed his astuteness in his adroit handling of an awkward situation with W.B. Yeats. In those early days of the state the government initiated a number of Commissions to sit on, deliberate and report on various aspects of the new emerging Ireland. One of those Commiss-ions set up dealt with the future cultural direction of the country. It was composed in the main of university professors, writers, artists and men known for their erudition. As a sop to public opinion a couple of TDs were put on, mostly men who were unlikely to rock the boat. Thady was one of those.

While the various academics droned on giving their pompous opinions the TDs were busily engaged in a competition of 'noughts and crosses'. They pursued their game quietly heedless of the verbose contributions of the others. On a particularly sultry day, after an unusually good lunch, the two speakers chosen by roster for the afternoon session were W.B. Yeats and Thady. At this time in his life Yeats was flirting madly with Indian mysticism and he spoke for an hour and forty minutes so obtusely that even the most erudite member could not understand him. When he sat down there was a sign of relief all round. The Chairman called on Thady to speak knowing that his contribution would be brief.

Thady collected the papers with the 'noughts and crosses', stood up and delivered himself of the most brilliant one-sentence speech I have ever heard: 'Mr Chairman,' he said, 'I have a lot of notes here on the subject in question but I don't intend to say anything for Mr Yeats took the words out of my mouth!'

And he sat down.

ACADEMY FOR THE POOR

Beside yon straggling fence that skirts the way
with blossomed furze unprofitably gay,
There in his noisy mansion skilled to rule
The village master taught his little school.

Our little school lay snugly nestled behind a growth of trees and bushes that sheltered it from the wild storms that swept in from the south-west. It was built as a one-roomed school in 1870 but later a movable partition was put in the centre to separate the Mistress, who taught Infants, First and Second class, from the Master who taught Third, Fourth, Fifth and Sixth.

At each gable-end there was a fireplace and in the wintertime lighting the fires was the first job on those cold mornings. There was no free fuel at the time so each pupil, or scholar as they were then called, had to bring one sod of turf to keep the fires going. And with an average of fifty or sixty scholars there was adequate fuel for the day.

The walls of the school were decorated with maps, charts, frames and other pedagogic paraphernalia, while over the fireplace and dominating the room hung a large picture of St Patrick, in his bright green pontificals, banishing the snakes from Ireland.

One rather unusual notice which appeared on the wall every day at 12 o'clock was a card with the printed words: RELIGIOUS INSTRUCTION. Some old rule obliged the master to display the notice when he was teaching the catechism. Each day when this card was hung up our three Protestant scholars left the room. How we envied them; no catechism, no questions to learn and answers, and an extra half-hour free. But we made them pay the price by baptising them regularly under the village pump on the way home and at the same time forcing them to say the Hail Mary.

The Master's son, or his Wayward Boy, as he was called, was up to every devilment, and he felt that baptism from the natural waters of the human body would be more spiritually efficacious. Whereupon he stood on the pump wall and administered this form of baptism on a young Protestant girl held by two companions. Nevertheless he was severely thrashed for this when the Master got to hear of it, but thrashings had little effect on him. In his view the devilment was always worth it.

The story had a strange sequel. Long years later the young girl so unusually baptised became a Catholic, joined a religious order, and ended up as its Mother General in Rome. There are those who say that the waters administered that day must have had some unusual spiritual components. But, out of respect, this is only said in the dark corners of hostelries.

There was no cloak-room of any description in our school. When we came in in the morning we threw what ragged caps or coats we had on the floor in the corner of the school and later retrieved them in a disorderly rush when classes were over.

About thirty yards behind the school, partly hidden by the bushes and trees, there were two crude privies – one for the boys and one for the girls. The toilet seats opened out on to the fields at the back and answering a call of nature could be quite hazardous in windy, snowy or wet weather. Unlike the home privies, it was the *Far East*, a missionary magazine, that hung from the nail on the walls. This was largely due to the influence of the Master who had a great devotion to the missionary efforts of the Church in China, and who was the local promoter of that worthy cause.

Here in this little school, generation after generation learned right from wrong, to read and write, add and subtract. Some few became famous, but for the most part the others lived out their lives in poverty and obscurity.

One of the most famous was Larry Lowry who emigrated to the United States and became a very wealthy man before he died. Astuteness blended with prudence and accuracy were his great virtues. He pretended to be thick, stupid and dense so that the master would not lean too heavily on him or question him too closely in class. His motto was: 'Always pretend to be a fool and then you'll fool the other fellow'. In school this worked magnificently.

Larry never used more words than were absolutely necessary and in his usually laconic sentences he said all there was to be said. Once the master taught a lesson on the Irish High Kings and in order to test Larry he named a number of High Kings. 'What,' he asked, 'have the following men in common – Niall of the Nine Hostages, Brian Boru, Malachy, Roderick O'Connor?'

Larry wasn't sure if they were all High Kings so he thought for a moment before giving the more accurate answer: 'They are all dead, sir!'

No one could dispute that.

For the most part however life was humdrum and only occasionally was its even tenor broken by Larry's witticisms.

I suppose the personality of every school is the personality of its master. I use the word 'Master' deliberately because he was never known as anything else – never Mr or Sir. It was 'Yes Master', 'No Master', the Master's house, the Master's dog, the Master's bicycle. It was a term of respect but with strong overtones of affection and love.

He was a tall well-built man with bushy eyebrows and receding hair. His face was stern yet kind. He was not a bully. He administered punishment where necessary, but he could always be lavish in his praise when deserved.

He had one or two blind spots. One of them was his son, to whom he always referred to as My Wayward Boy. I suppose every one of us has some kind of a cross to bear in life and in the Master's case it was his Wayward Boy.

There was no devilment to which this lad was not up to.

Robbing orchards and stealing fruit were the mildest. They were just kid's games. He was always just one step ahead of the police. They were never able to catch him red-handed at anything.

When he was an altar-boy considerable quantities of the wine went missing, especially at Christmas time. It was then noticed that quite a number of geese and turkeys in the village were staggering around blind drunk. An examination of the meal on which they fed showed it to be saturated with alcohol. Here matters came to a head when a farmer brought a sow to the boar for service. It seems as if the Wayward Boy had got to the boar first, who had just had a dinner of yellow meal well soused in altar wine. When the great moment came the boar couldn't stand properly and kept falling off his beloved and missing the target, until he finally fell dead asleep on top of the unfortunate sow who was by now anxious for a bit of diversion but who eventually attacked and bit the farmer in a fit of frustration. This led to angry words between the two farmers, which eventually led to blows and eventually the police had to be called in to separate them.

On another occasion the inspector was due at the school and the Wayward Boy estimated that it would be late afternoon before he reached the class. He decided to act at lunchtime when the assistant lady teacher cooked a meal of tea, scones and boiled eggs for the inspector. Some kind of purgative was surreptitiously slipped into the inspector's tea pot and shortly after lunch-time he felt the need to absent himself to the back. This happened more and more frequently as the afternoon went on and in the end the inspector felt it better to go home early. He could not examine the Wayward Boy's class. All he could do was give them full marks.

Another of the Wayward Boy's specialities was attending to newly married couples on their first nights. Now in those days there were no honeymoons. The happy couple went to town for the day and came home on the last bus.

The Wayward Boy would watch the house until he'd see the candle had been quenched in the bedroom. He would then knock loudly on the door until he heard himself coming down and then he ran. This would happen several times during the night so that the poor newly-weds never got a proper chance to exercise their conjugal rights on the happiest night of their lives.

Nevertheless he always managed to keep within the law, to keep one step ahead of the police or at worst avoid getting caught. There was a constant string of complaints poured into the police or his father who sadly claimed that he would come to no good and that he brought nothing but disgrace and heartbreak to the family. In one public outburst in school the Master declaimed: 'You blackguarding scamp. I forecast for you that not alone will you see the inside of every jail in Ireland but somewhere in South America the hemp is growing that will make the rope that Pierpoint, the public hangman, will hang you with. You have broken my heart and disgraced our family and you well deserve whatever happens to you'.

But sometimes God writes straight with crooked lines and events did not turn out quite as the master forecast.

Our Master was one of the old school of educators who believed that the final end of all education is the happiness of human beings. It was as simple as that. But human happiness in a wind-swept poverty-stricken countryside has many aspects, not the least being material welfare. The pupils had to be taught to add and subtract, divide and multiply, so that they could buy and sell without fear of being swindled at a fair or other merchandising event. He deviated from the text books in that he related the problems set in the books to a form of daily life to which they could relate. If a sow had fourteen bonhams and three died, how many were left? If one farmer had six bullocks and another had three times as many, how many had the second farmer? If you were hired by a ganger to work on the road at two shillings and nine pence a day, how much would you get on Saturday evening? If a bank of turf measured ten yards by five yards and you had to pay a shilling per square yard, how much would the lot cost you? He taught us to measure the acreage of fields, the size of linoleum for a room, the number of scallops to thatch a house, the amount of lime required to whitewash the outside of a house.

He taught us how to read and write and spell so that we could make out what was written in the weekly paper or in *The Far East* or in a pension book or on a dog licence so that we would not mistake it for a boar licence. To be literate meant that we could read the American letter that came from our emigrants every month with a few dollars in it, and if things were bad we could compose a letter asking for a little more.

For those few of us who had advanced a little more Dickens, the Brontes and Jane Austen were discarded after the British left and were replaced by Kickham, Sheehan, Mrs Pender and Michael O'Hanrahan. So too did Shelley, Keats, Wordsworth make way for Pádraig Colum, Pádraig Pearse, Thomas MacDonagh and a host of other Irish poets whose writings expressed the people to themselves. I especially remember the thrill of first learning Colum – every word he wrote had a meaning in the world around us, the world we knew and understood:

> *Oh men from the fields*
> *Come gently within*
> *Tread softly, softly*
> *Oh men coming in.*

or

> *Oh to have a little house,*
> *To own the hearth, and stool and all!*
> *The heaped up sods upon the fire,*
> *The pile of turf against the wall!*

All out literary efforts were in some way related to life as we saw it all around us. We could identify with the hurling in Sheehan's *Glenanaar*, the wren-boys in *Knocknagow*, the tinkers in Carleton's *Traits and Stories*, and above all we identified with Power's *Kitty the Hare*, that master storyteller who brought to life ghosts, banshees, fairies, devils and angels and whose stories usually ended with a quatrain:

> *There's my story*
> *And come what may*
> *Put on the kettle*
> *And make the tay.*

Our religion was also brought to life in a setting we understood. Capharnaum, Galilee and Nazareth were identified with local villages and Christ walked our roads, milked our cows, cut our turf just as he did in reality. I recall vividly an occasion he spoke to us of St Peter's denial.

The setting was a fair in a local town and Christ was after being arrested by the Black-and Tans. This servant girl, or skivvy as the master called her, told the Black-and-Tans that Peter was one of them. Peter turned on her in somewhat non-apostolic language: 'you dirty tinker's bitch. All belonging to you were tramps who hadn't an arse to their britches, and who died in the poor-house . You never had anything in your life except a bag of straw to lie on and a skillet of yella meal to eat, and you lived in the corner of the kitchen with a sow and a litter of bonhams'.

Although the skivvy threw the charge in his face a couple of times he convinced the Black-and-Tans that the skivvy was a slut and a liar and they let him go.

All this was completely real to us and we had no trouble identifying with it. Years later the old man admitted to me that he sought above all to get his pupils to *identify* with Christ – a profound theological principle, whether he knew it or not. Did he not say, 'Learn of me for I am meek and humble of heart'.

But the master's abiding passion was his love of wild life. He believed that there was an underlying unity in all life, man, animal, bird, tree or fish. He often told us that man is no more than 50,000 years old but that all other forms of life are several billion years old. Why then should man have domination over the others? We are only 'blow-ins' on this earth. We have dominated by cruelty and aggression. We have brought nothing but misery to the world, to each other and to nature.

He conceded that hunger gave one the right to kill but nothing gave one the right to kill for sport. Fox-hunting and coursing he abhorred. He effectively organised the farmers against fox-hunting packs so that there was nowhere outside their own lands they could hunt. He had a theory which he expounded at length that the faces and mouths of fox-hunting people became uncannily like the horses' arses, and when we did get an opportunity of comparing them we really did notice quite a resemblance.

In spring he spoke to us of the mating birds, or courting couples, as he called them. He identified their amorous antics so that we could detect at once when there was a bit of fun in the air. He encouraged us to watch them especially when they nested and each day we had to report on the progress of the hatching and the growth of the little birds.

All this had the effect of giving us the feeling that all nature was part of our family and our instincts were to help and fondle rather than to kill. It was a beautiful upbringing to be at one with nature and with God. Even after half a century I can still identify with all living things.

He also took a special interest in those few pupils who had more than ordinary talent. It was not unusual to see four, five or six ragged youths sitting around his kitchen table on weekends preparing for some scholarship examination. From those ragged urchins ultimately came an archbishop, a cabinet minister, an army colonel, a superintendent of the police, a county manager and several senior civil servants. All this was given free.

Then one day after a lifetime of labour he retired. Subscriptions were solicited all around for a presentation – a suite of furniture and an illuminated address.

The schoolhouse was bedecked for the occasion, crowded with his ex-pupils. The canon made the presentation. A reporter and photographer from the local paper were present. It was his finest hour when he humbly thanked them all.

The illuminated address was set in a large gilt-edged frame. It was a masterly blend of affection and cliches:

We desire to place on record our esteem and admiration for your sterling qualities as a teacher during all those years you were with us. You came amongst us when the general conditions of the school and plot were in a bad state. You faced your task of improving those conditions with all the energy and ability at your command with a result that today we find a vast change from the conditions that then existed.

Your chief aim at all times was to further the interests of those under your charge. Each succeeding year pupils from your school obtained the highest marks in religious and secular examinations. Those aspiring to positions of trust always received from you valuable assistance and advice.

You helped to instil into the minds of the pupils a love of everything Irish, everything that is racy of the soil. The teaching of our native language always found its rightful place in your curriculum. The support of Irish manufactured goods was encouraged and the promotion of Gaelic games fostered to a high degree.

Local worthy objects claimed your best attention. You never neglected the wants of the destitute and needy. Ample evidence is available of your sincerity in times of trying circumstances. When awkward situations arose you faced them unflinchingly regardless of the consequences.

And now on your well-deserved retirement we wish you 'ad multos annos' with many long years of a happy and peaceful life.

The only dark shadow on that wonderful day was the absence of his Wayward Boy. He had run away from school and was reported missing. All the other members of the family were present. But the old man took it calmly. 'Every man is given a cross to carry in his life,' he said. 'Mine is my eldest son. We must accept what the good Lord sends us. He is a plain common blackguard. I don't know where we got him. On both sides our families were always respectable'.

He lived a long life after his retirement but his weekend kitchen sessions continued. When he reached his mid-nineties he began to look forward to his hundredth year. The prize here was a letter from the President of Ireland and a cheque for £5.

But when he reached his ninety-seventh year he made a momentous decision. 'Three years more is too long to wait for a five-pound note,' he said. The day after he remained in bed and a week later he died. On his death certificate the cause of death was given as simply 'old age'.

He was waked in traditional style – snuff, drink and clay pipes. The day after, his funeral was of massive proportion. Hundreds of his past pupils came from all parts of the country to pay their last respects. The graveyard was crowded with mourners.

They laid his coffin in a simple grave and when the last of the mourners had left the grave-diggers filled it in and left too. All was now silent.

I slowly wandered into the graveyard alone. I stood over the flower bedecked mound with conflicting emotions welling up within me. My whole lifetime was somehow in that grave. Then something snapped and I burst into uncontrollable sobs. The tears poured down my face and I could do nothing to stop them. They poured on and on ... so well they might ... you see, I was his Wayward Boy.

Epilogue

On the marble floor of Siena Cathedral there are seven mosaics depicting the course of man's life – much the same as Shakespeare's seven ages of man. They were created in the fifteenth century by Antonio Federighi and restored in the nineteenth century by Alessandro Franchi. They have a message for those who heed them well.

The first is that of a child happily pursuing a butterfly; then a young boy with a book under his arm making his way to school; next comes an adolescent with a falcon on his arm – going hunting as flowers spring up everywhere he walks; then comes the young man with the light of love in his eyes; and after him the mature man full of wisdom and respectability; then an old man in a fur coat feeling his rosary beads, and finally in the centre of a circle composed of the other six comes the last – a decrepit, bent old man fumbling his way towards a tomb.

I have passed most of these stages although I do not agree that the final stages are anything as devastating as Federighi portrays them. They can be the most wonderful stages of all, when the passions of youth have subsided, the illusions and arrogance of manhood have given way to a mellowness and serenity – and disappointment and pain have blended into a stoical acceptance.

I hope I never see myself bent over shuffling towards the grave. I would much prefer to walk briskly towards it with my head held high and the lilt of a song in my heart. The grave is in reality the gateway to the fullness of life – the dark passage after which comes the light of eternity, the answer to every question that has baffled me during the course of my life.

I write as an old man who is well into the twilight of his

days. I have climbed the mountain of life and the broken fragments of my failures and sorrows are strewn on the rugged path behind me. Beyond there are signs of a dawn observed by a morning mist. What is out there I do not know.

So many of those I loved have dropped out on the way. Will I ever meet them again? What is beyond the grave – they know the answer, I don't.

I confess to a certain morbid curiosity but I have one great consolation. I will be judged by a God, and not by a human, who is unlikely to run me in for all eternity because I liked the sparkle of wine or the flash of a pair of pretty legs. Like Baudelaire I have loved beauty but when I found it, it was not always beautiful.

I have very little to show after a long life, but I also ask for very little – a few dogs, a few books, birds and nature and a few companions like Lahy. Surely He will grant me that.

***

John M. Feehan put the final touches to My Village – My World *[excluding the Epilogue] on Tuesday 21 May. He had chest pains that night and went to hospital the following morning. He died around 1.55a.m. on Saturday 25 May 1991. When the manuscript was being prepared for publication two scraps of paper were found with the above material written on them – they seemed like a fitting epilogue.*

He is now on another great journey to a different life with his beloved family and friends who have gone before him and who undoubtedly were waiting joyfully for him – there must be great talk wherever they are now – the Wayward Boy has returned home.

In one of his books he wrote 'when nature makes a man of true greatness she throws away the mould' – ní bheidh a leithéid ann arís.